Black Historical Figures

Public Activist

Copyright © 2022 by Every Dollar Countz LLC
All rights reserved. This book or any portion thereof
may not be reproduced or used in any manner whatsoever
without the express written permission of the publisher
except for the use of brief quotations in a book review.

TABLE OF CONTENTS

11 JOHN LEWIS

107 KAMALA HARRIS

155 MICHELLE OBAMA

3	Harriet Tubman	67	Angela Davis	131	Nelson Mandela
11	John Lewis	75	Fred Hampton	139	Rosa Parks
19	Shirley Chisholm	83	Jesse Jackson	147	Thurgood Marshall
27	Nat Turner	91	Dorothy Height	155	Michelle Obama
35	Fannie Lou Hammer	99	Malcolm X	163	Martin Luther King Jr
43	Frederick Douglass	107	Kamala Harris	171	Sojourner Truth
51	Ella Baker	115	Medgar Evers	179	Huey Newton
59	Barack Obama	123	Colin Kaepernick	187	Iyanla Vanzant
				195	Claudette Colvin

These Workbooks are geared to intrigue, inspire and motivate you to want to learn more about these Black Historical Figures(BHFs) and others. Also to do more research on your own. We know this isn't all the history of these individuals. We want you to do some of the research also. We try to be as accurate as possible during our research. If there are some stories or questions that aren't as stated, please contact us at info@wegonnalearntoday.com.

Harriet Tubman

Harriet Tubman

March 1822 – March 10, 1913
ABOLITIONIST

LEFT BLANK ON PURPOSE

Harriet Tubman

Harriet Tubman

Harriet Tubman

Harriet Tubman

Harriet Tubman

Harriet Tubman

Directions: read the bio below and answer the following questions.

Hi, my name is Araminta Ross. I was born in March 1822 in Dorchester County, MD. I was born a slave because my mother was a slave. She gave me the nickname "Minty." When I was an adolescent, I suffered a severe head injury, which brought on painful headaches and seizures. When I was about 24, I married John Tubman and changed my name to Harriet Tubman. In 1849, I made my escape to Pennsylvania by traveling by the North Star and trying to avoid slave catchers who were eager to collect rewards for fugitive slaves. Over the years, I went on about 13 missions to rescue approximately 70 enslaved people, including my family and friends, using the network of antislavery activists and safe houses that was known as the Underground Railroad. During that time, I also worked for the Union Army, first as a cook and nurse and then as an armed scout and spy. I was also the first woman to lead an armed expedition in the war.

1. What was my mother's nickname for me?
   A. Moses
   B. General Tubman
   C. Minty
2. What year did I escape being a slave?
   A. 1849
   B. 1848
   C. 1844
3. What branch did I work for?
   A. Marine Corps
   B. Navy
   C. Union Army

Directions: Answer the questions, to solve the crossword puzzle. You can use the internet if you get stuck on any question.

Across
5) Harriet worked with leading _____ of the day, like John Brown.
7) Harriet suffered a _____ head injury as an adolescent.
8) One of Harriet's nicknames was _____.

Down
1) Harriet was buried with _____ honors in Fort Hill Cemetery in New York.
2) After the Fugitive Slave Act of 1850 was passed, Harriet helped guide slaves to _____.
3) Harriet helped find a cure for _____.
4) Harriet was the first woman to lead an armed assault in the _____.
6) Harriet never lost a single one of the many slaves she guided to___.

Directions: When Harriet was born there were twelve slave states and twelve free states. Below can you figure out what was the border line between these states. Write the corresponding number on the map for those states.

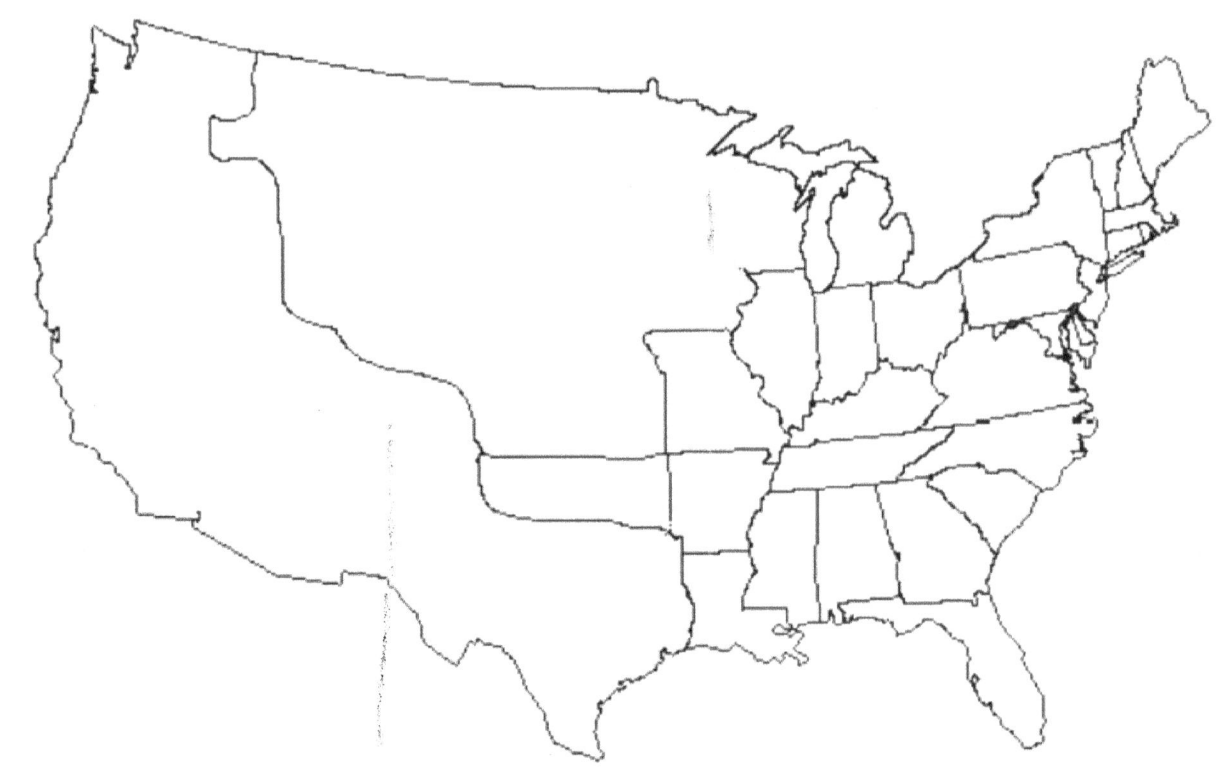

Labels

1) Illinois
2) Missouri
3) Ohio
4) Kentucky
5) New Jersey
6) Virginia
7) Indiana
8) Pennsylvania
9) Maryland
10) Delaware

Directions: Unscramble the words below about Cicely. See if you can get the bonus word.

BONUS WORD

Unscramble Words

1) yvsearl **2)** nacdaa **3)** iplahhaiPdel
4) ablniiitsoot **5)** tcosu **6)** soems
7) piosmnheyra **8)** mniyt **9)** akrQuse

Directions: This is the WGLT Challenge. Solve the cryptogram. As the puzzle solver, you need to find which number belongs to which character. And this can be pretty challenging! You will need to match the number with the letter. There are some letters given to you below. This will help you solve the other words and unlock more characters. **Good Luck.**

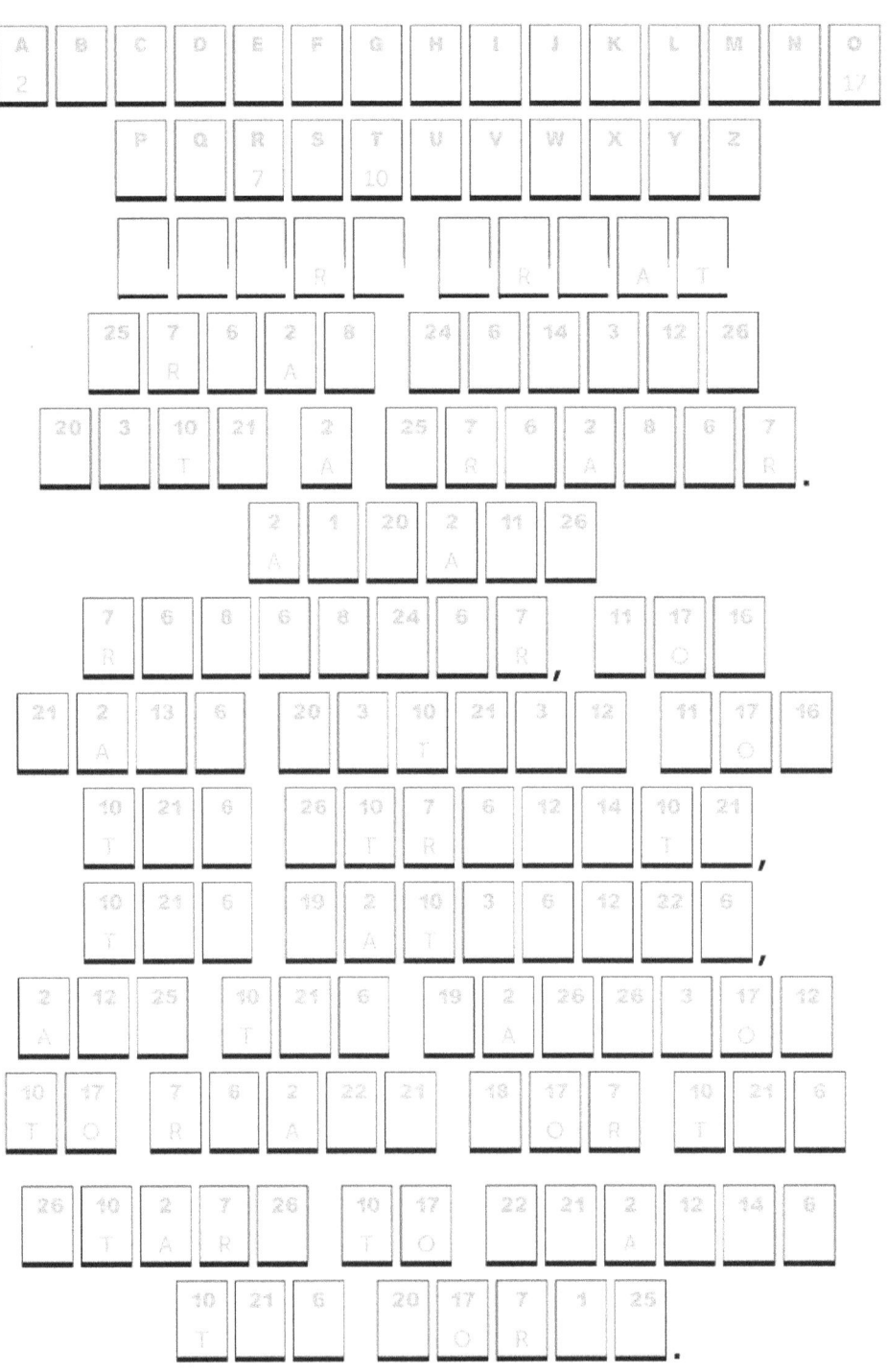

John Lewis

John Lewis

February 21, 1940 – July 17, 2020
CIVIL RIGHTS ACTIVIST/POLITICIAN

LEFT BLANK ON PURPOSE

John Lewis

John Lewis

John Lewis

John Lewis

John Lewis

John Lewis

Directions: read the bio below and answer the following questions.

Hi, my name is John Lewis. I was born on February 21, 1940, in Pike County, AL. From a young age, I always wanted to be a preacher. When I was 15, I gave my first public sermon. Three years later, I met Martin Luther King, Jr. I graduated from the American Baptist Theological Seminary in Nashville, TN and was ordained as a Baptist minister. I earned a bachelor's degree in religion and philosophy from Fisk University, I also became a member of the Phi Beta Sigma fraternity. As a student, I became an activist during the civil rights movement. I organized sit-ins at segregated lunch counters in Nashville. I was also one of the 13 original Freedom Riders. I was the chairman of the Student Nonviolent Coordinating Committee (SNCC) from 1963 to 1966. I helped organize the 1963 March on Washington. In 1965, I led the first of three Selma to Montgomery marches across the Edmund Pettus Bridge. In 1986, I became a member of the U.S. House of Representatives.

1. What was my degree in?
    A. Education
    B. Computer Science
    C. Religion and Philosophy
2. What is the name of my fraternity?
    A. Alpha Phi Alpha
    B. Omega Phi Psi
    C. Phi Beta Sigma
3. What branch of the government did I represent?
    A. U.S. House of Representatives
    B. Senate
    C. Executive

Directions: Find the words associated with John's life and career.

U	V	M	S	R	E	D	I	R	M	O	D	E	E	R	F	D	L
C	U	N	Z	N	I	L	Z	E	A	J	D	S	C	M	E	F	V
D	I	K	S	F	O	Z	A	Q	O	D	A	C	E	M	N	Y	X
O	T	L	T	H	U	N	Z	Z	I	W	M	J	O	M	M	P	L
I	P	F	H	M	C	Z	V	M	U	Z	R	C	S	O	B	R	F
A	O	U	G	X	O	Q	W	I	C	K	R	K	N	U	I	R	L
N	L	Y	I	J	U	N	O	I	O	A	D	S	C	G	G	N	C
I	I	O	R	D	B	S	C	E	T	L	T	B	C	E	S	P	L
I	T	W	L	U	S	Z	S	I	N	W	E	O	X	Y	I	W	R
P	I	F	I	X	E	O	C	L	I	N	S	N	O	J	X	J	R
L	C	Q	V	O	V	P	S	U	W	D	Y	Y	T	L	X	H	Q
B	I	A	I	D	A	E	E	C	S	S	O	U	M	E	N	P	E
R	A	Q	C	R	U	U	L	T	D	Q	M	W	X	F	H	T	O
K	N	E	T	W	S	V	M	Y	R	E	M	O	G	T	N	O	M
J	C	Y	X	X	V	C	A	S	Y	S	O	C	B	Z	R	Z	A
X	R	C	G	O	O	D	T	R	O	U	B	L	E	E	U	Q	L
H	W	Q	N	O	N	J	M	T	K	Y	Q	G	A	L	K	Y	Y
L	E	G	G	E	Q	G	X	S	Z	I	J	S	V	P	V	M	O

Find These Words

DEMOCRATICPARTY   CIVILRIGHTS   SELMA
NONVIOLENT   FREEDOMRIDERS   SNCC
BIGSIX   GOODTROUBLE   MONTGOMERY
POLITICIAN

15

Directions: Put the labels under the right Branch of Government

LEGISLATIVE	EXECUTIVE	JUDICIAL

Labels

1) Make Laws
2) Signs Laws
3) Decides if laws are constitutional.
4) Approves presidential appointments.
5) Veto's Laws
6) Appointed by the President.
7) Two Senators from each state.
8) Appoints federal judges.
9) There are nine Justices.
10) Number of congressmen based on population of each state.
11) Elected every four years.
12) Can overturn rulings by other judges.
13) Pardons people.

Directions: Read and answer the questions below. There are clues in the puzzle to help you. Try and solve the cryptic message.

Clue for cryptic message: John worked for them.

Questions

1) John was a _____ speaker during the 1963 March on Washington.

2) John was the _____ of the Student Nonviolent Coordinating Committee (SNCC)

3) John was a _____ Rider, an organization, which challenged the non-enforcement of the law, which stated that segregated public buses were unconstitutional.

4) John received the highest civilian _____ of the United States, the Presidential Medal of Freedom.

5) John was a devoted advocate of the philosophy of _____.

6) John helped lead more than 600 _____ protestors across the Edmund Pettus Bridge in Selma, Alabama, on March 7, 1965.

7) John was one of the "_____" leaders of groups who organized the 1963 March on Washington.

8) John was reelected _____ times to serve in the United States House of Representatives for Georgia's 5th congressional district.

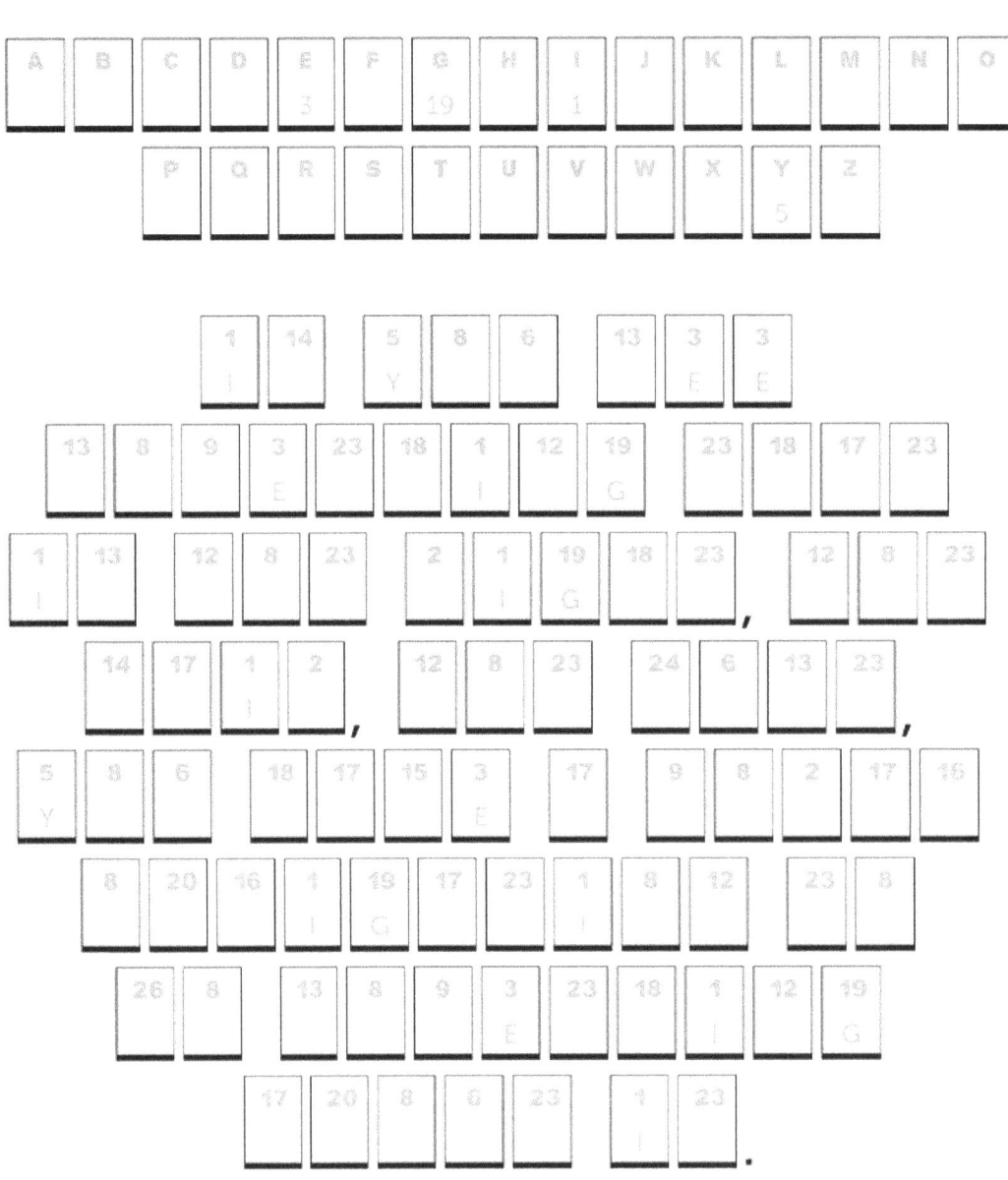

November 30, 1924 – January 1, 2005
POLITICIAN

LEFT BLANK ON PURPOSE

Shirley Chisholm

Shirley Chisholm

Shirley Chisholm

Shirley Chisholm

Shirley Chisholm

Shirley Chisholm

Directions: read the bio below and answer the following questions.

Hi, my name is Shirley Chisholm. I was born on November 30, 1924, in Brooklyn, NY. When I was 5, I went to stay with my grandmother in Barbados. I came back to the US when I was about 10, but by that time, I had picked up a West Indian accent that would follow me for the rest of my life. I attended Girls' High School in Brooklyn. I then attended Brooklyn College, where I earned a Bachelor of Arts in Sociology. While there, I also became a part of the Delta Sigma Theta sorority. After college, I became a teacher's aide at the Mt. Calvary Child Care Center in Harlem from 1946 to 1953. I earned my Master of Arts in Childhood Education from the Teachers College of Columbia University in 1951. In 1968, I became the first Black woman to be elected to the United States Congress for seven terms (1969–1983). In 1972, I became the first Black candidate for a major-party nomination for president of the United States and I was the first woman to run for the Democratic Party's nomination.

1. What was Bachelor degree in?
    A. Childhood Education
    B. Sociology
    C. Computer Science
2. What year did I get elected to Congress?
    A. 1968
    B. 1972
    C. 1983
3. How old was I when I went Barbados?
    A. 10
    B. 3
    C. 5

Directions: Answer the questions, to solve the crossword puzzle. You can use the internet if you get stuck on any question.

Across
1) Shirley was a _____ school teacher.
2) Shirley graduated from _____ University.
4) Shirley was inducted into the National Women's _____ in 1993.
5) Shirley was on the _____ Committee while in Congress.
6) Shirley was he first African-American woman to declare her _____ for President of the United States.
7) Shirley was a founding member of the Congressional _____.

Down
1) Shirley has a _____ named after her.
3) Shirley was the first Black woman in _____.

23

Directions: Read and answer the questions. These are Presidential Powers.

Possible Answers

budget	congress	Marines	nuclear weapons
president	bills	supreme court	legislative
vetoed	Senate	impeached	supports
armed forces	treaties	laws	judicial
executive	vice president	House	abolishes

1) The president can propose new _____.

2) The vice president _____ the president and helps him or her carry out their job.

3) The president is the head of the _____ and can decide whether or not to use _____.

4) If the _____ can't do his or her job, the vice president takes over.

5) The president makes _____ with other countries.

6) The _____ is the president of the Senate.

7) The president and vice president are part of the _____ branch.

8) Any bill passed by Congress can be _____ by the president.

9) The vice president can appear before the _____ on behalf of the president.

10) If the president is accused of doing something wrong, they can be _____.

Directions: Unscramble the words below about Shirley. See if you can get the bonus word.

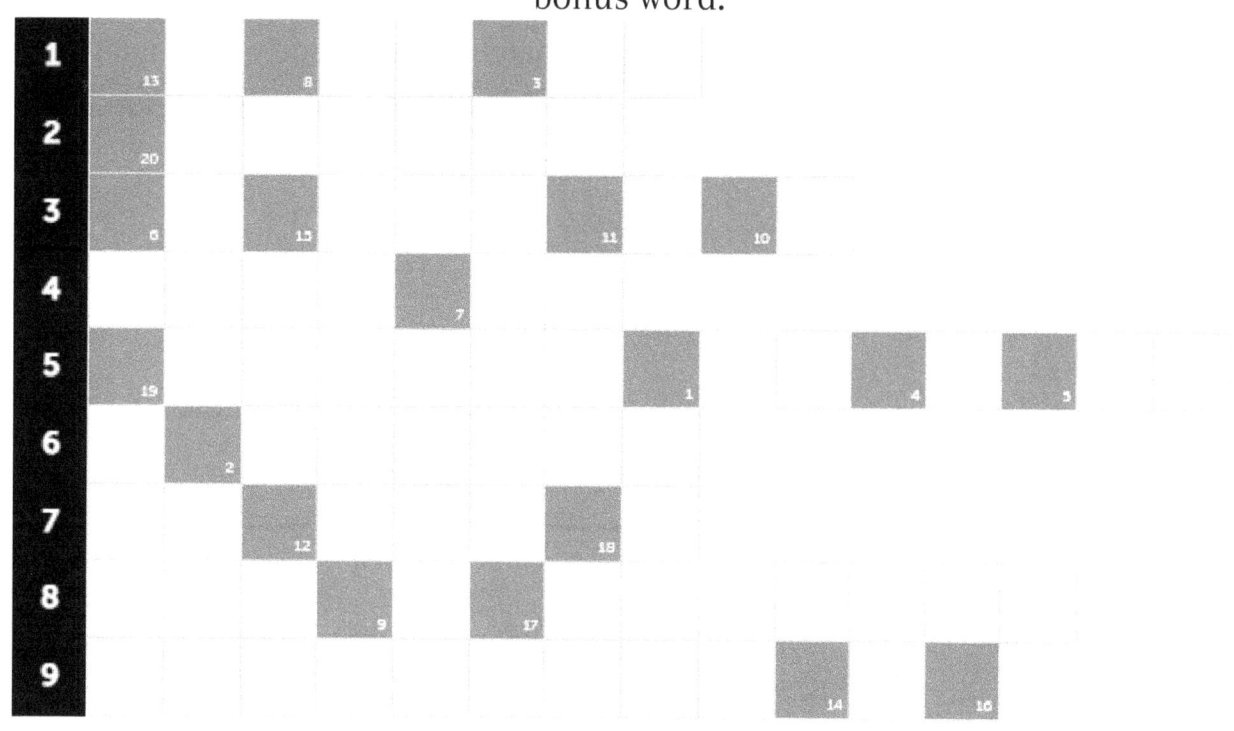

BONUS WORD

Unscramble Words

1) crnsoseg   **2)** rkonewy   **3)** mictocdaer
4) srnuery   **5)** spseietaerndorg   **6)** ryolnbok
7) iumlCaob   **8)** msestybtelasa   **9)** mtpefvaersro

25

Directions: This is the WGLT Challenge. Solve the cryptogram. As the puzzle solver, you need to find which number belongs to which character. And this can be pretty challenging! You will need to match the number with the letter. There are some letters given to you below. This will help you solve the other words and unlock more characters. **Good Luck.**

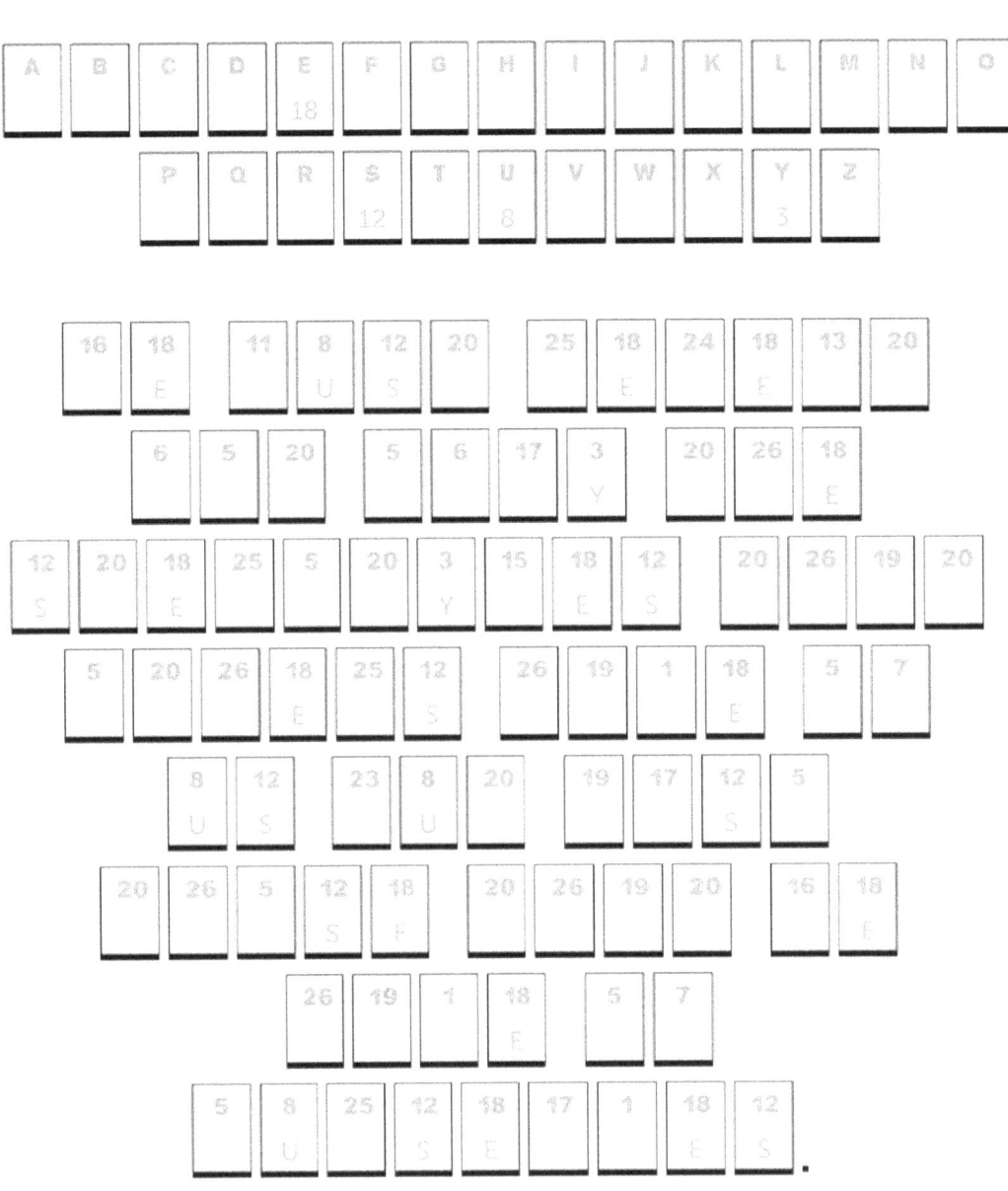

Nat Turner

Nat Turner

October 2, 1800 – November 11, 1831
PREACHER

LEFT BLANK ON PURPOSE

Nat Turner

Nat Turner

Nat Turner

Nat Turner

Nat Turner

Directions: read the bio below and answer the following questions.

Hi, my name is Nat Turner. I was born on October 2, 1800, in Southampton County, VA. I was born a slave and when I was young, I displayed "uncommon intelligence" and was taught to read and write. My deeply religious grandmother nurtured my spiritual development. Growing up, I regularly read the Bible and preached to my fellow enslaved people. When I was 21, I escaped, but "the Spirit appeared to me and said I should return to the service of my earthly master." On August 21, 1831, I began a rebellion with several trusted fellow slaves, a few more than 70 enslaved people and free Black people, some of whom were on horseback. The rebels traveled from house to house, freeing enslaved people and killing many white people whom they encountered. In the wake of the rebellion, several states passed laws that made it illegal to teach African Americans how to read or write. My revolt contributed to the radicalization of American politics that helped set the United States on its course toward the Civil War.

1. Who turned me on to reading the Bible?
    A. Mother
    B. Grandmother
    C. Father
2. How old was I when I escaped?
    A. 18
    B. 15
    C. 21
3. Why did we rebel?
    A. To learn ho to read and write
    B. To get married
    C. To escape slavery

Directions: Find the words associated with Nat's life and career.

```
S L P O A Z S L A V E H O L D E R G
V J F X G G W J B H K B X K I Y P I
S B Q D Q W N O I T A T N A L P U K
N Q S E S P I L C E R A L O S D K D
E V F D X G J T M C K K D G G C P U
L E N B Y Q B X D Q L U V M Z E K J
E Q Z V R E B E L L I O N Z Q D A H
H X Z D T J V S M G T K L E T U N V
. V B U U A A Z A I H S B A F C J Z
T U W C L G N I U Q N S B W R A C G
S K J S C I N A T J C I G Y X T L A
T U N B L I L G W L E O S X B E B U
N E F Z G M V C Z R B F U T C D Y O
U G V R R P H J W X S U V O E V M B
O M I T S S N O I G I L E R E R Z N
M V P B V E K P X B Z Y B L P M Y K
G Q U G D P D O Z B O R D V X I W D
L M J W U X V C G X K C U Q D L Z U
```

Find These Words

REBELLION   ENSLAVED   MINISTER
SOLARECLIPSE   MOUNTST.HELENS   EDUCATED
RELIGION   PLANTATION   SLAVEHOLDER
VIRGINIA

Directions: Read and answer the questions some words may be used more than once. How the Branches work.

Judicial	six	Vice President	Senate
Legislative	one	The House of Representatives	President
Speaker	two	Executive	four

1) What two groups make up Congress. _____

2) What are the three branches of government.

_____

3) The _____ is the leader of the house of representatives.

4) The _____ holds the trial for a government person who is being impeached.

5) The Senate has _____ members to represent each state.

6) The _____ is the leader of the senate.

7) The _____ determines if a government person should be impeached.

8) Members in the senate serve _____ years.

9) Members in the house of representatives serve _____ years.

10) The _____ servers for four years.

11) Why do you think it is important to have different branches of government?

Directions: Read and answer the questions below. There are clues in the puzzle to help you. Try and solve the cryptic message.

Clue for cryptic message: Nat was one of these.

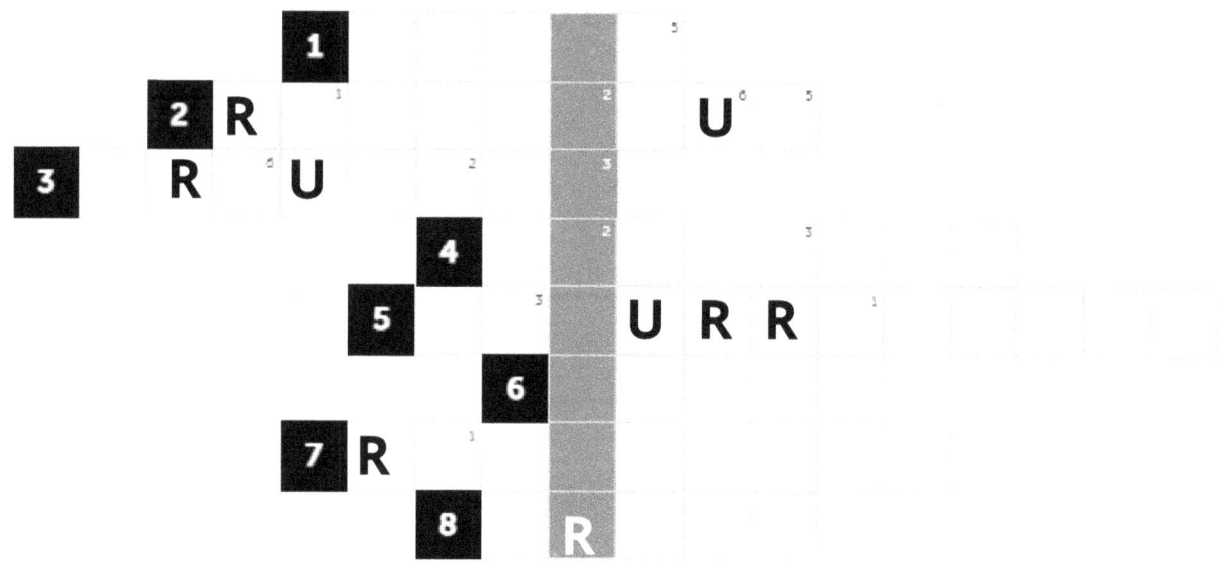

Questions

1) Nat has had books, music and _____ created about him.
2) Nat was very _____ and spent a lot of time studying the bible.
3) Nat believed that Mount St. Helens _____ and cast of a hazy light to be another sign to continue with the rebellion.
4) Nat believes he was _____ chosen to lead the rebellion.
5) Nat was tried and convicted of 'conspiring to rebel and making an _____.
6) The General Assembly passed legislation making it unlawful to _____ reading and writing to either enslaved or free Blacks.
7) After the slave _____ there were laws passed to make it illegal for African Americans to be taught to read or write.
8) Nat learned to read and _____ was considered to be an intelligent person despite him being a slave.

Directions: This is the WGLT Challenge. Solve the cryptogram. As the puzzle solver, you need to find which number belongs to which character. And this can be pretty challenging! You will need to match the number with the letter. There are some letters given to you below. This will help you solve the other words and unlock more characters. **Good Luck.**

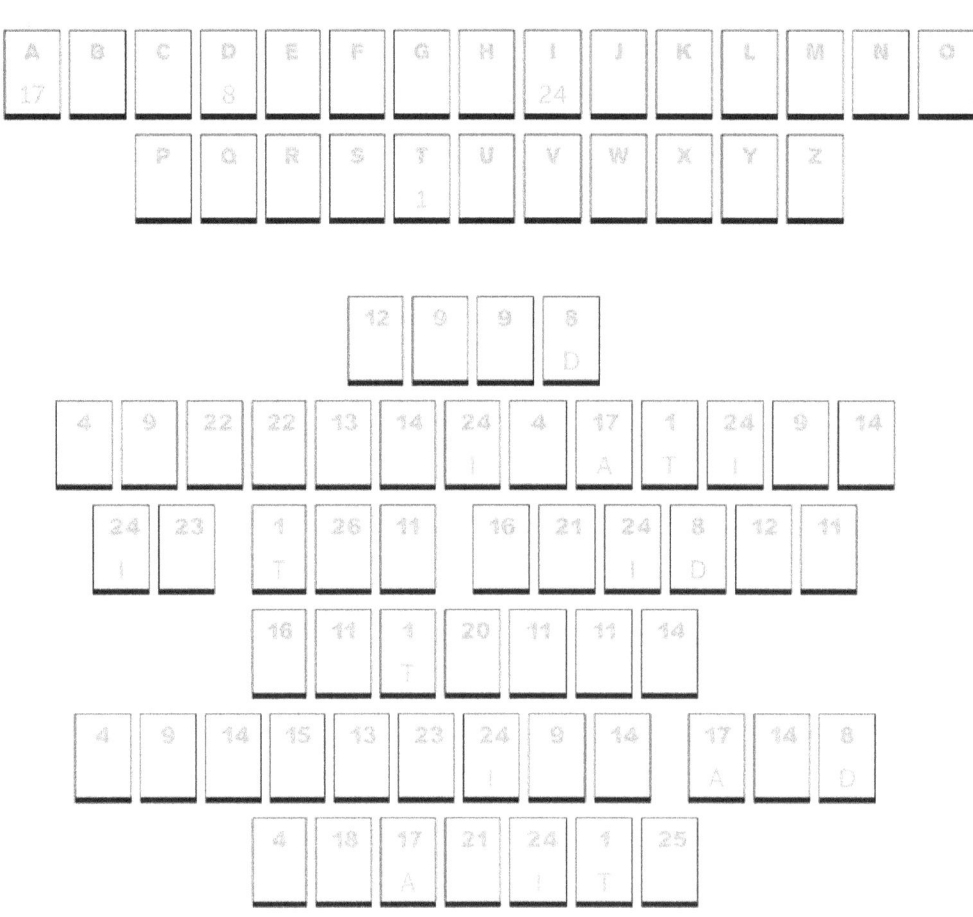

Fannie Lou Hamer

Fannie Lou Hamer

October 6, 1917 – March 14, 1977
WOMEN RIGHTS ACTIVIST

Fannie Lou Hamer

Fannie Lou Hamer

Fannie Lou Hamer

Fannie Lou Hamer

Fannie Lou Hamer

Fannie Lou Hamer

Directions: read the bio below and answer the following questions.

Hi, my name is Fannie Lou Townsend. I was born on October 6, 1917, in Montgomery County, MS. Around age 12, I had to leave school to support my aging parents. I continued to develop my reading and interpretation skills during Bible studies at church. In 1945, I married Perry "Pap" Hamer, who was a tractor driver on the Marlow plantation and remained there for the next 18 years. On August 31, 1962, seventeen other Black people and I attempted to vote but failed a literacy test, which meant that I was denied this right. I was fired by my boss for trying to register to vote. The next month, I was shot at fifteen times by racists in a drive-by shooting. I eventually passed the test and registered to vote on January 10, 1963. In 1964, I helped co-found the Mississippi Freedom Democratic Party (MFDP) to prevent the regional all-white Democratic Party's attempts to stifle African American voices and to ensure that there was a party for all people that did not stand for any form of exploitation or discrimination (especially towards minorities).

1. How old was I when I left school?
   A. 15
   B. 12
   C. 10
2. What year did I register to vote?
   A. 1962
   B. 1963
   C. 1961
3. What party did I represent?
   A. Independent
   B. Republican
   C. Democrat

Directions: Answer the questions, to solve the crossword puzzle. You can use the internet if you get stuck on any question.

Across

5) Fannie was the co-founder and vice-chair of the Freedom _____ Party

7) Fannie joined an integrated _____ from Mississippi at the 1968 Democratic National Convention.

8) Fannie was a field _____ for voter registration and welfare programs for SNCC.

Down

1) Fannie traveled around the South to _____ black people about voting rights.

2) Fannie fought to expand _____ rights for African Americans.

3) Fannie organized Mississippi's _____ Summer in 1964.

4) Fannie dedicated herself to the _____ movement.

6) Fannie was a _____ of the National Women's Political Caucus.

Directions: Read and circle the right answers. The 15th Amendment.

The Fifteenth Amendment (Amendment XV) to the United States Constitution prohibits the federal government and each state from denying or abridging a citizen's right to vote "on account of race, color, or previous condition of servitude." It was ratified on February 3, 1870, as the third and last of the Reconstruction Amendments. The Democratic Party in the southern states adopted new state constitutions and enacted "Jim Crow" laws that raised barriers to voter registration. This resulted in most black voters and many poor white ones being disenfranchised by poll taxes and discriminatory literacy tests, among other barriers to voting, from which white male voters were exempted by grandfather clauses.

1) What was the 15th Amendment?
An amendment to the U.S. Constitution that abolished slavery
An amendment to the U.S. Constitution that addressed the issue of citizenship
An amendment to the U.S. Constitution that banned discriminatory voter registration practices
An amendment to the U.S. Constitution that gave women the right to vote

2) What was the 'Jim Crow" laws?
A required dress code for African Americans.
A secret code used by former slaves.
Laws that limited the social and working rights of African Americans.
None of the answers are correct.

3) What law put into place rules to insure people of all races had the right to vote?
Voting Rights Act
Stamp Act
Social Security Act
Equal Protection Act
Right to Privacy Act

4) What is it called when a certain group of people are kept from voting?
Intimidation
Disenfranchisement
Literacy
Bipartisanism
Prohibition

Directions: Unscramble the words below about Fannie. See if you can get the bonus word.

BONUS WORD

1	2	3	4	5	6	7	8	9	10	11	12	13

Unscramble Words

1) wmigntoerhs   **2)** ovrest   **3)** mdecaort
4) isisismppsi   **5)** gssraotosr   **6)** toumr
7) yaetquli   **8)** sieecrttlayt   **9)** aopxltl
10) lehflamfoa

41

Directions: This is the WGLT Challenge. Solve the cryptogram. As the puzzle solver, you need to find which number belongs to which character. And this can be pretty challenging! You will need to match the number with the letter. There are some letters given to you below. This will help you solve the other words and unlock more characters. **Good Luck.**

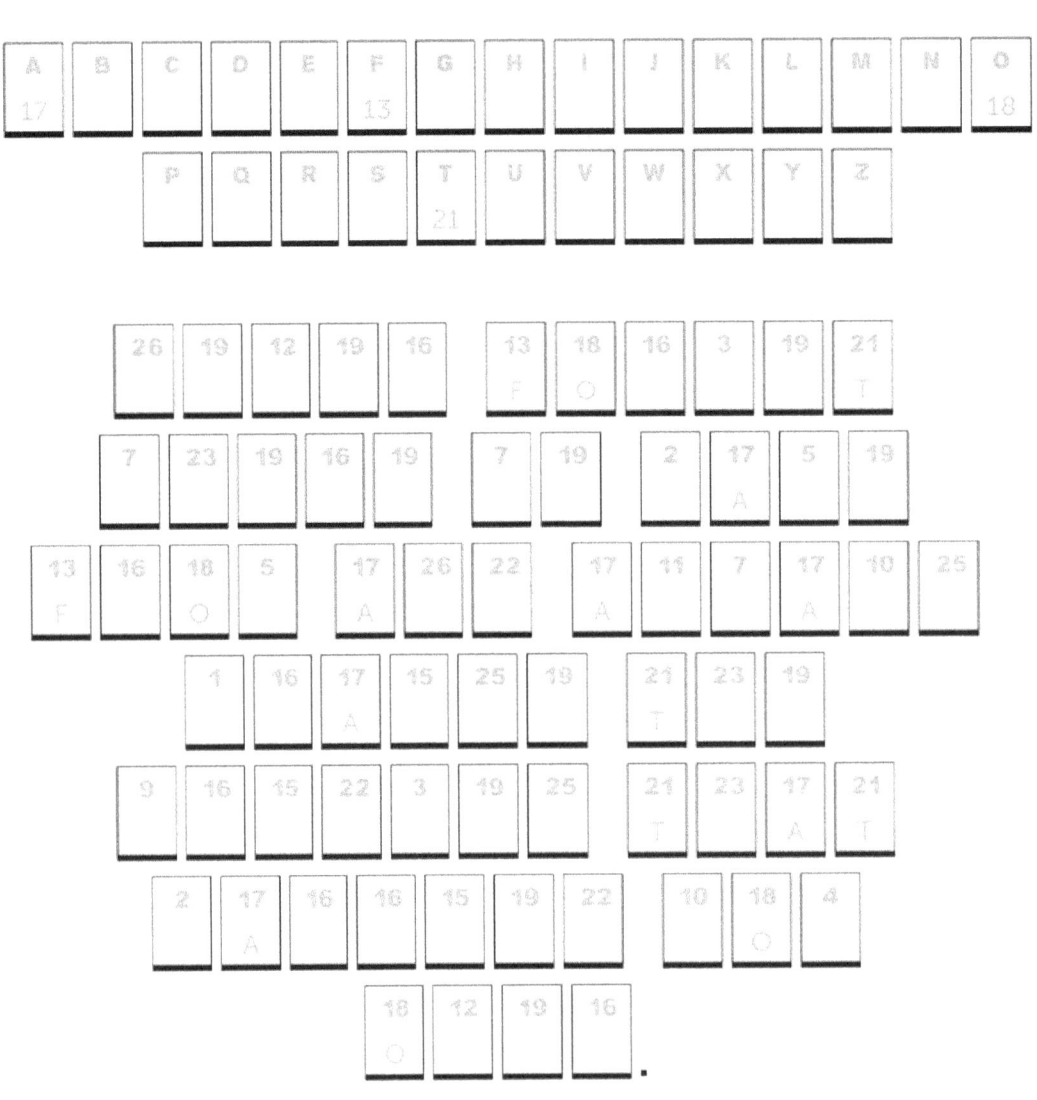

Frederick Douglass

Frederick Douglass (cursive)

February 1818 – February 20, 1895
ABOLITIONIST

43

LEFT BLANK ON PURPOSE

Frederick Douglass

Frederick Douglass

Frederick Douglass

𝓕𝓻𝓮𝓭𝓮𝓻𝓲𝓬𝓴 𝓓𝓸𝓾𝓰𝓵𝓪𝓼𝓼

𝓕𝓻𝓮𝓭𝓮𝓻𝓲𝓬𝓴 𝓓𝓸𝓾𝓰𝓵𝓪𝓼𝓼

𝓕𝓻𝓮𝓭𝓮𝓻𝓲𝓬𝓴 𝓓𝓸𝓾𝓰𝓵𝓪𝓼𝓼

Directions: read the bio below and answer the following questions.

Hi, my name is Frederick Augustus Washington Bailey. I was born on February 1818, in Talbot County, MD. I was born into slavery, but around age 12, my master's wife started teaching me the alphabet. She stopped after her husband made her change her mind. I learned to read from white children in the neighborhood and by observing the men with whom I worked. In 1838, I successfully escaped by boarding a northbound train that belonged to the Philadelphia, Wilmington and Baltimore Railroad. I then changed my surname to Douglas after having read the poem "The Lady of the Lake" by Walter Scott, in which two of the principal characters have the surname "Douglas." I also founded The North Star, which was an abolitionist newspaper. In 184, I attended the Seneca Falls Convention to speak on women's right to vote. I consulted with President Abraham Lincoln during the Civil War and helped influence the Emancipation Proclamation.

1. What year did I escape slavery?
   A. 1840
   B. 1818
   C. 1838
2. What was the name of my newspaper?
   A. Washington Post
   B. New York Times
   C. The North Star
3. What president did I help influence?
   A. Andrew Johnson
   B. Abraham Lincoln
   C. James Buchanan

Directions: Find the words associated with Frederick's life and career.

```
P Q S V S F O X B H W J C Z V I T K
V F E K A L E H T F O Y D A L E H T
U K I N E S A L Y U M M H I Y L H R
S I S A R W V V A H X L W Z L Z A A
R C Q M H V N Q E A R P M U B Q N J
M F R S V G V R Y R V E H R T Q N D
T A M E H V V K M S Y D W H S Z A U
G L F T I U Z B R F O A C R I L M X
H N N A M A W J J O J B Q S N J U A
P G I T E G T R W L W H O E O N R Y
Q I I S C I I A I W V W U Z I I R M
V U T C X W I L E T D J B O T F A R
T B K B U R E A K Z E M W C I Q Y A
T H E N O R T H S T A R U F L D A N
P W I T Y F K A U Z O Z A X O M Y O
N I C P H B S R X J K T M B B G Y I
Z I A M L C W Q G F T Q C P A P T N
V Z Y N O S D O O W G R E T R A C U
```

Find These Words

ABOLITIONIST   WRITER   STATESMAN
SLAVERY   VICTORIAWOODHULL   UNIONARMY
ANNAMURRAY   CARTERGWOODSON   THENORTHSTAR
THELADYOFTHELAKE

Directions: Read and answer the questions with a word or sentence from the word bank. The Thirteenth Amendment.

Thirteenth Amendment states: Neither slavery nor involuntary servitude, except as a punishment for crime whereof the party shall have been duly convicted, shall exist within the United States, or any place subject to their jurisdiction. **Abolitionism:** The fight to end slavery in the United States began in the late 1700s. People who wanted to end slavery were called abolitionists because they wanted to "abolish" slavery. Rhode Island was the first state to abolish slavery in 1776, followed by Vermont in 1777, Pennsylvania in 1780 and many other northern states soon after. **Emancipation Proclamation:** During the Civil War, President Lincoln issued the Emancipation Proclamation on January 1, 1863. This freed the enslaved in the Confederate States that were not under Union control. Although it did not immediately free all of the enslaved, it set the groundwork for the Thirteenth Amendment.

WORDS

Prohibitionists	Abraham Lincoln	World War II
World War I	Abolitionists	Made slavery illegal
Civil War	Guaranteed religious freedom	George Bush
Slavers	Jimmy Carter	Spanish-American War
Guaranteed women the right to vote		Federalists
Legalists		Outlawed the sale of alcoholic drinks

T1) What were people who wanted to outlaw slavery called?

2) What president issued the Emancipation Proclamation?

3) What war was fought in the United States largely over the issue of slavery?

4) What did the Thirteenth Amendment do?

Directions: Read and answer the questions below. There are clues in the puzzle to help you. Try and solve the cryptic message.

Clue for cryptic message: Frederick did this a lot.

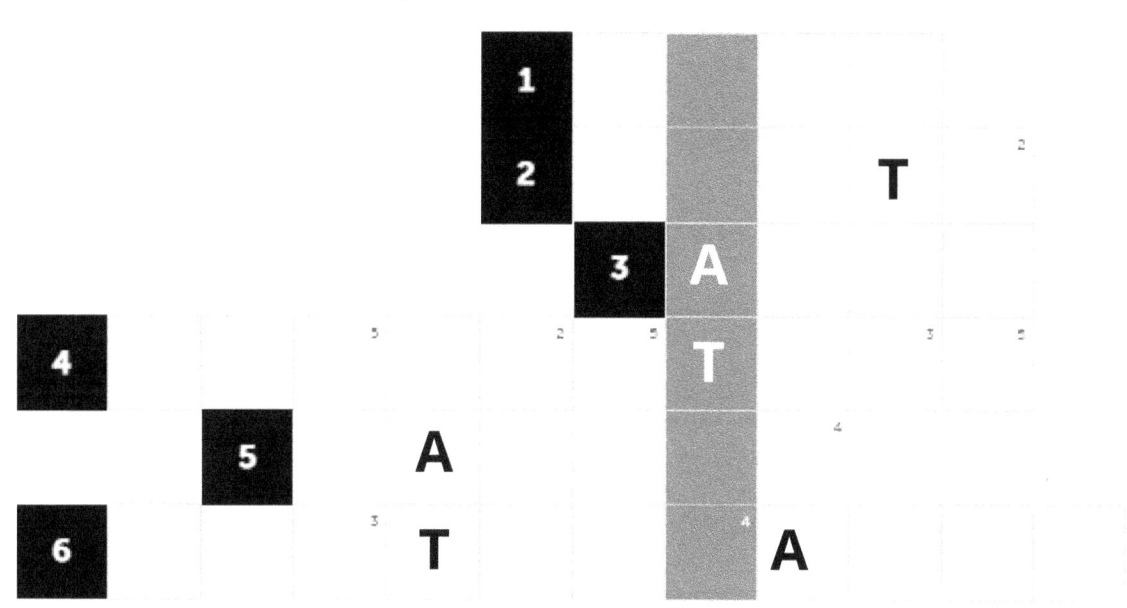

Questions

1) Frederick took the surname Douglass from a famous _____.
2) Frederick taught himself how to read and _____.
3) Frederick helped enlist free black men to fight in the Union _____.
4) Frederick was the only African American to attend the First Women's Rights _____.
5) Frederick escaped from slavery dressed as a _____.
6) Frederick was the most _____ American of the 19th century.

Directions: This is the WGLT Challenge. Solve the cryptogram. As the puzzle solver, you need to find which number belongs to which character. And this can be pretty challenging! You will need to match the number with the letter. There are some letters given to you below. This will help you solve the other words and unlock more characters. **Good Luck.**

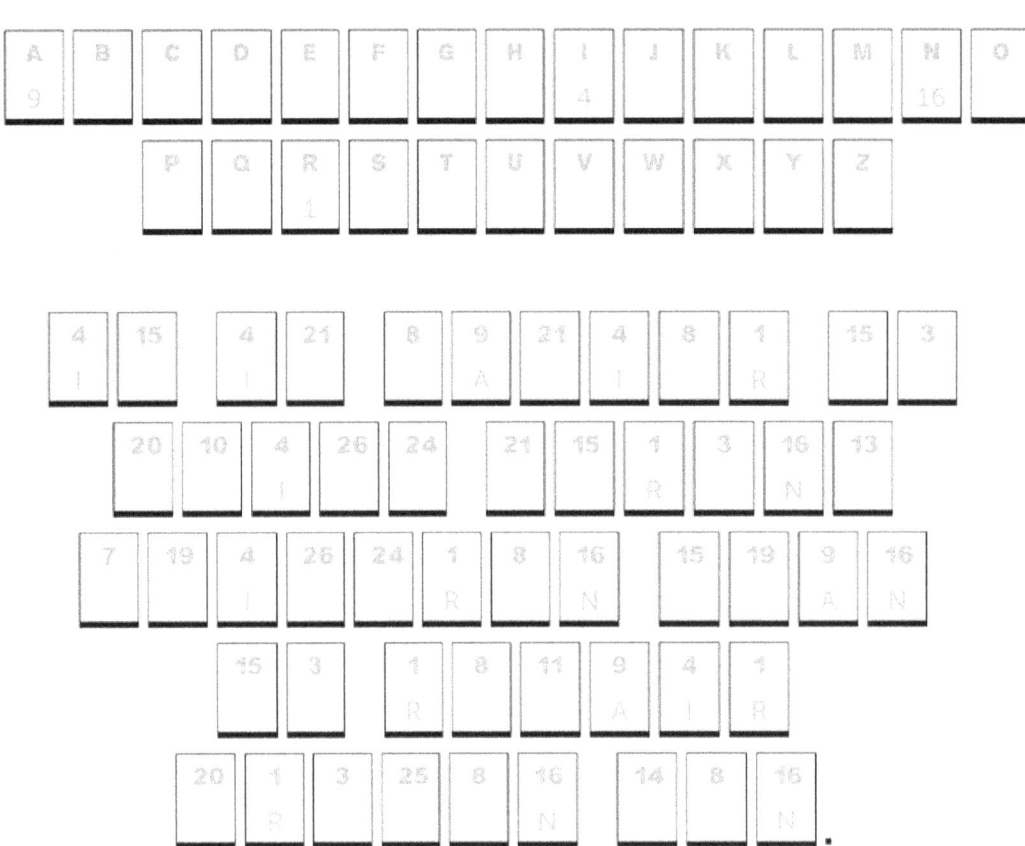

Ella Josephine Baker

Ella Josephine Baker

December 13, 1903 – December 13, 1986
CIVIL RIGHTS ACTIVIST

LEFT BLANK ON PURPOSE

Ella Josephine Baker

Ella Josephine Baker

Ella Josephine Baker

Ella Josephine Baker

Ella Josephine Baker

Ella Josephine Baker

Directions: read the bio below and answer the following questions.

Hi, my name is Ella Josephine Baker. I was born on December 13, 1903, in Norfolk, VA. At 15, I attended the high school academy of Shaw University in Raleigh, NC. I continued my college education at Shaw and graduated as valedictorian in 1927. I joined the National Association for the Advancement of Colored People (NAACP) in 1938 and I also helped with Martin Luther King, Jr.'s fledgling Southern Christian Leadership Conference (SCLC). Although sexism within the SCLC barred me from becoming the organization's permanent executive director, I was indispensable to the SCLC's success between 1957 and 1960. I organized the Student Nonviolent Coordinating Committee (SNCC) in 1960 and this group helped create the Freedom Riders and Freedom Summer. I worked alongside these civil rights leaders of the 20th century: W. E. B. Du Bois, Thurgood Marshall and Martin Luther King, Jr. I also mentored many emerging activists, such as Diane Nash, Stokely Carmichael and Bob Moses, who were leaders of the SNCC.

1. What does NAACP stand for?
   A. National Association for the Advancement of Colored People
   B. National Association for All Colored People
   C. National Association for Any Colored Person
2. What did I graduate college as?
   A. Salutatorian
   B. Valedictorian
   C. Summa Cum Laude
3. What does SNCC stand for?
   A. Students Not Coordinating Color
   B. Students New Color Committee
   C. Student Nonviolent Coordinating Committee

Directions: Answer the questions, to solve the crossword puzzle. You can use ...et if ...

Across

3) Ella was one of the great _____ leaders of the 20th century.
5) Ella was the primary _____ and strategist for SNCC.
7) Ella helped the student _____ Coordinating Committee (SNCC) launch the Freedom Rides in 1961.
8) Ella nickname was "____" which loosely translates as 'someone who passes on knowledge to the next generation' in Swahili.

Down

1) Ella was _____ of her class at Shaw University in Raleigh, NC.
2) Ella helped organize the _____ Freedom Democratic Party (MFDP).
4) Ella worked for the NAACP as a _____.
6) Ella was the first full-time _____ of the Southern Christian Leadership Conference (SCLC).

Directions: Read and answer the questions. Ella founded this movement. Student Nonviolent Coordinating Committee (SNCC) sought to coordinate youth-led nonviolent, direct-action campaigns against segregation and other forms of racism. SNCC members played an integral role in sit-ins, Freedom Rides, the 1963 March on Washington and such voter education projects as the Mississippi Freedom Summer. Although SNCC, or 'Snick' as it became known, continued its efforts to desegregate lunch counters through nonviolent confrontations, it had only modest success. In May 1961, SNCC expanded its focus to support local efforts in voter registration as well as public accommodations desegregation.

1) What didn't the SNCC do?

A. Sit-ins

B. Freedom Rides

C. Fight

2) What was the nickname of SNCC?

A. Snail

B. Snick

C. Stow

3) What did SNCC expand its efforts to support?

A. Bailing people out of jail

B. Running for public office

C. Voter registration

Directions: Unscramble the words below about Ella. See if you can get the bonus word.

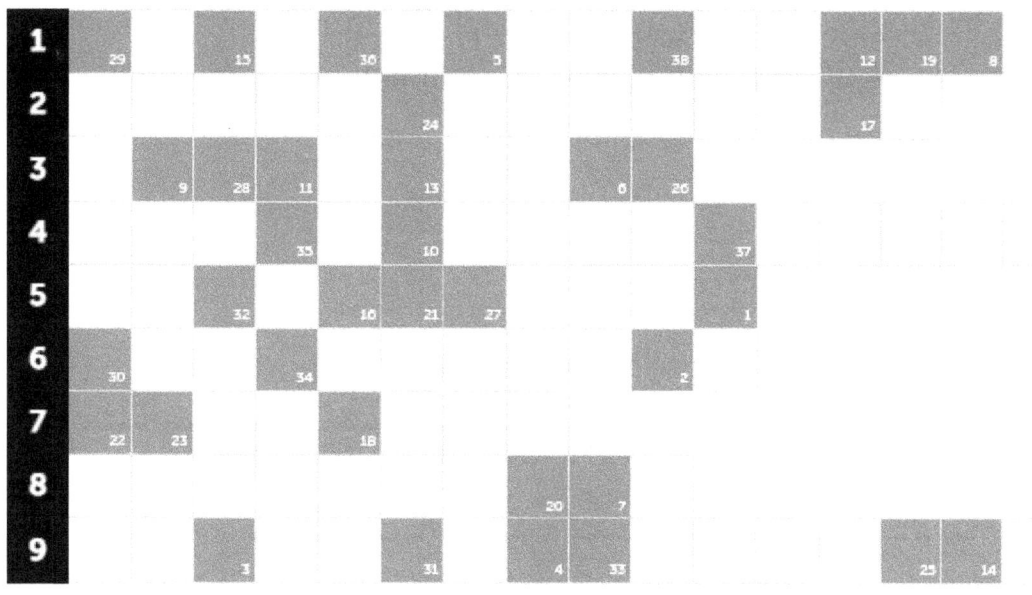

BONUS WORD

Unscramble Words

1) natdeegsorserip
2) rutwevishnisya
3) lteononvni
4) tminrergkhjltarnui
5) gsrtumiahnh
6) istgcivlhir
7) iocterrd
8) rgrootsssa
9) ourhmldsgroalhta

Directions: This is the WGLT Challenge. Solve the cryptogram. As the puzzle solver, you need to find which number belongs to which character. And this can be pretty challenging! You will need to match the number with the letter. There are some letters given to you below. This will help you solve the other words and unlock more characters. **Good Luck.**

Barack Obama

Barack Obama

August 4, 1961 - PRESENT
44th U.S. President

LEFT BLANK ON PURPOSE

Barack Obama

Barack Obama

Barack Obama

Barack Obama

Barack Obama

Barack Obama

Directions: read the bio below and answer the following questions.

Hi, my name is Barack Hussein Obama II. I was born on August 4, 1961, in Honolulu, HI. My first name means "one who is blessed" in Swahili. I graduated in 1979 from Punahou School, which is an elite college preparatory academy in Honolulu. I graduated from Columbia University with a degree in political science. I also attended Harvard Law School and graduated magna cum laude. I was the first African American editor of the Harvard Law Review. I was elected to the Illinois Senate in 1996. During my time there, I sponsored and led the unanimous, bipartisan passage of legislation to monitor racial profiling. This legislation required police to record the races of the drivers whom they detained and made Illinois the first state to mandate the videotaping of homicide interrogations. I was elected to the U.S. Senate in 2004. On November 4, 2008, I won the presidency. I became the first African American to be elected president. Along with Warren G. Harding and John F. Kennedy, I am one of the only U.S. senators to move directly from the U.S. Senate to the White House.

1. What Law school did I go to?
    A. Columbia
    B. Yale
    C. Harvard
2. In 2008 I was the first African-American to do what?
    A. Become U.S. Senator
    B. Become U.S Congressman
    C. Become U.S President
3. What State did I become a senator of?
    A. Hawaii
    B. Illinois
    C. New York

Directions: Find the words associated with Barack's life and career.

```
C Q N Q B F D S T Y S S E W M D M R
O O A O C L N Y F E E O D Y T P Z B
M B L N B V P Q N N W I D F D R L I
M H K O I E N X A L L E Z G W E K I
U L A Z O I L T B L L W X F J S A Z
N I B L B H O P I A U T H O R I O J
I Q C G A R C N E X B X F P A D O Z
T I O M F W O S N A B N O B A E T X
Y U L W Q I P E W M C L C N I N C T
O D U A S E C R N A I E V A T T G S
R R M O M B J I O T L X P S M P H Z
G C B K E B I E I F E D Y R V I T D
A F I C B R O C E S E D R P I I K Z
N Q A G N P I U R Q Z S Z A G Z V Q
I M O X W A F Y N Y O N S B V E E T
Z U P V N R O H Y V G V Q O R R W A
E W K P B D E B L G K Z O F R X A J
R L I I D U F J S E G C V T K E H H
```

Find These Words

ILLINOIS   HARVARDLAWSCHOOL   AUTHOR
COMMUNITYORGANIZER   LAWPROFESSOR
NOBELPEACEPRIZE   PRESIDENT   SENATOR
COLUMBIA   POLITICIAN

63

Directions: read and answer the questions. **Questions about the Senate.** Use the internet to help you.

1) **How many representatives in the Senate does each state have?**

1

2

4

2) **How old do you have to be to become a member of the Senate?**

30

24

18

3) **Who is considered the President of the Senate?**

Speaker of the House

Secretary of State

Vice President of the United States

4) **How long is the term of a member of the Senate?**

2 years

5 years

6 years

5) **What branch of government does the Senate belong to?**

Executive

Judicial

Legislative

6) **Which of the following is a special power of the Senate?**

They ratify treaties with foreign governments

They appoint a governor for each state

They determine if laws are constitutional

7) **How many members are there currently in the Senate?**

50

200

100

8) **What is it called when a Senator tries to delay the vote on a bill by giving a really long speech?**

Veto

Filibuster

Ratification

Directions: Read and answer the questions below. There are clues in the puzzle to help you. Try and solve the cryptic message.

Clue for cryptic message: Barack's name.

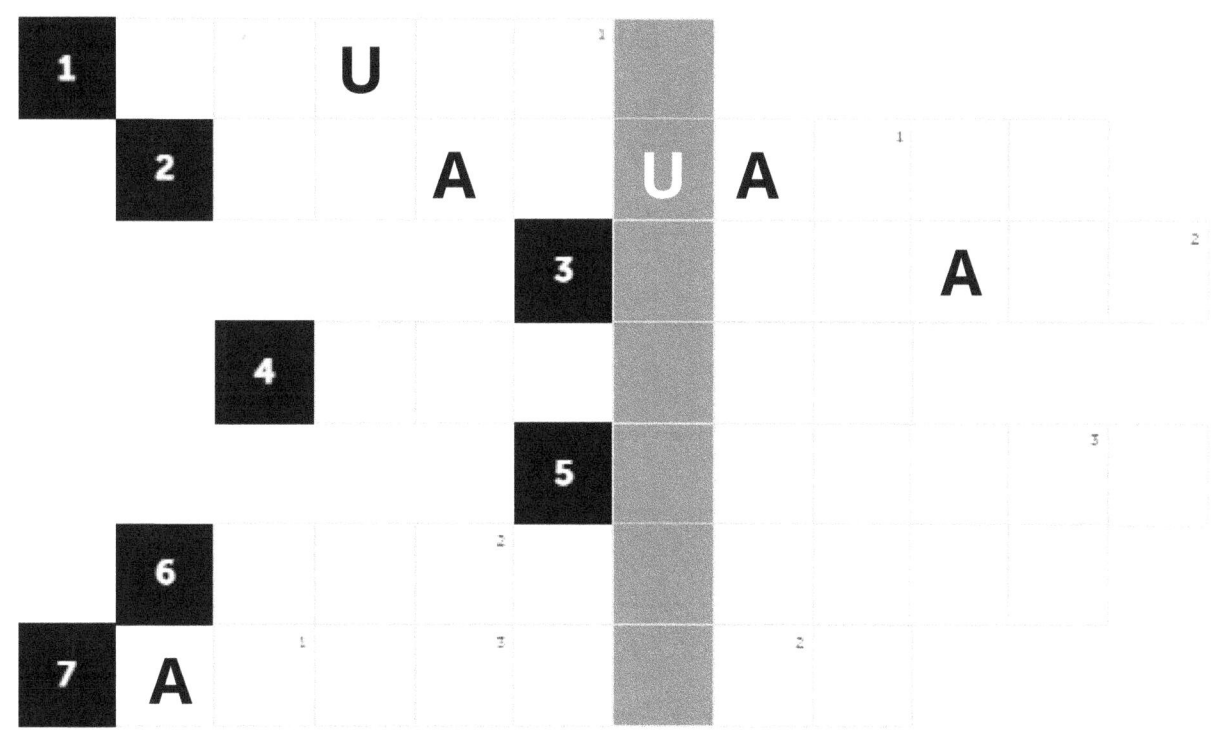

Questions

1) Barack was the forty-____ president of the United States and he served two terms.
2) Barack _____ from Columbia University with a degree in political science.
3) Barack was elected to the Illinois _____ representing Chicago's south side neighborhoods.
4) Barack was named Time magazine's "____ of the Year." twice.
5) Barack was the first African-American _____ of the Harvard Law Review.
6) Barack was the first African-American _____ of the United States
7) Barack use to work as a civil rights _____.

Directions: This is the WGLT Challenge. Solve the cryptogram. As the puzzle solver, you need to find which number belongs to which character. And this can be pretty challenging! You will need to match the number with the letter. There are some letters given to you below. This will help you solve the other words and unlock more characters. **Good Luck.**

Angela Davis

Angela Davis

January 26, 1944 - PRESENT
POLITICAL ACTIVIST

LEFT BLANK ON PURPOSE

Angela Davis

Angela Davis

Angela Davis

Angela Davis

Angela Davis

Angela Davis

Directions: read the bio below and answer the following questions.

Hi, my name is Angela Davis. I was born on January 26, 1944, in Birmingham, AL. I attended Elisabeth Irwin High School in Greenwich Village. There, I was recruited by a communist youth group, Advance. I was awarded a scholarship to Brandeis University in Waltham, MA. In 1965, I graduated magna cum laude and was a member of Phi Beta Kappa. I also earned a master's degree from UCLA in 1968, as well as a Ph.D. in philosophy from Humboldt University in East Berlin. I was an active member of the Communist Party and I participated in the formation of the Black Panther Party and the transformation of the Student Nonviolent Coordinating Committee (SNCC). I was falsely accused of murder and kidnapping. I was placed on the FBI's most-wanted list. I spent eighteen months in jail, which led to the "Free Angela Davis" campaign and the creation of the Angela Davis Legal Defense Committee. In response, John Lennon and Yoko Ono wrote "Angela," and the Rolling Stones wrote "Sweet Black Angel."

1. What is my highest level of education?
   A. Bachelor Degree
   B. Masters Degree
   C. Ph. D
2. What crime was I accused of?
   A. Theft
   B. Murder
   C. Communist
3. What society did I become a member of after I graduated?
   A. National Honor Society
   B. Phi Beta Kappa
   C. Phi Theta Kappa

Directions: Answer the questions, to solve the crossword puzzle. You can use the internet if you get stuck on any question.

Across

4) Angela was a follower of notable leftist _____ Herbert Marcuse.
7) Angela criticized the 1995-million-man march for its _____ of women.
8) At one time, Angela was named to FBI's Top 10 _____ fugitives list.

Down

1) Angela life's work was to educate people on and discuss issues regarding racial discrimination, _____ and the criminal justice system.
2) Angela was awarded the _____ Prize from the Soviet Union in 1979.
3) Angela was inducted into the National Women's _____.
5) Angela was acquitted of _____ in 1972.
6) Angela traveled extensively and lived in _____ and East Germany.

Directions: Read and answer the questions. 13th Amendment facts. Use the internet to help you.

1) The Supreme Court ruled that the military draft (when the government forces people to join the military) was not a violation of the Thirteenth Amendment.
True or False

2) What war was fought in the United States largely over the issue of slavery?
War of 1812
Spanish-American War
Civil War

3) What were people who wanted to outlaw slavery called?
Prohibitionists
Abolitionists
Federalists

4) What year did the state of Mississippi finally ratified the thirteenth amendment.
1975
1985
1995

5) The amendment still allows for slavery as a punishment for a crime.
True or False

6) What did the Thirteenth Amendment do?
Guaranteed women the right to vote
Guaranteed religious freedom
Made slavery illegal

7) What percentage of people living in the South in the mid-1800s were slaves?
20%
50%
90%

5) What president issued the Emancipation Proclamation?
Abraham Lincoln
John Adams
George Washington

Directions: Unscramble the words below about Angela. See if you can get the bonus word.

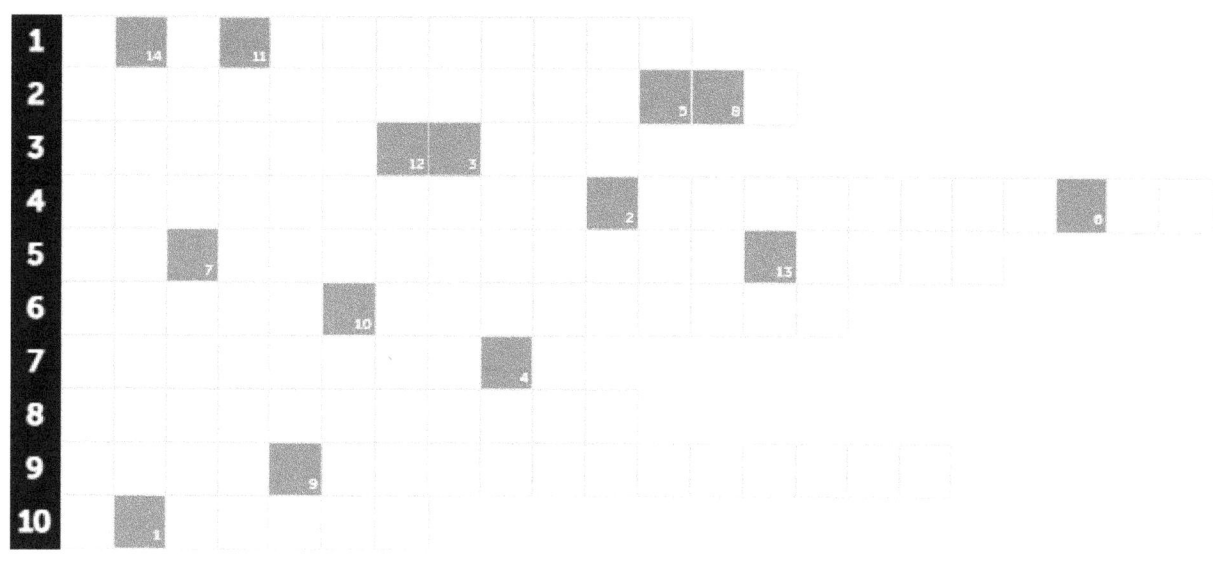

BONUS WORD

Unscramble Words

1) alydtiinlhem
2) rmteasbreceHur
3) nytaaemegrs
4) oylrinciavfuisrieafnto
5) riitilectaceanscsr
6) ipnaelircepenez
7) alfaemofhl
8) prslhopoehi
9) ttvcaasipoicitill
10) ahrlcos

Directions: This is the WGLT Challenge. Solve the cryptogram. As the puzzle solver, you need to find which number belongs to which character. And this can be pretty challenging! You will need to match the number with the letter. There are some letters given to you below. This will help you solve the other words and unlock more characters. **Good Luck.**

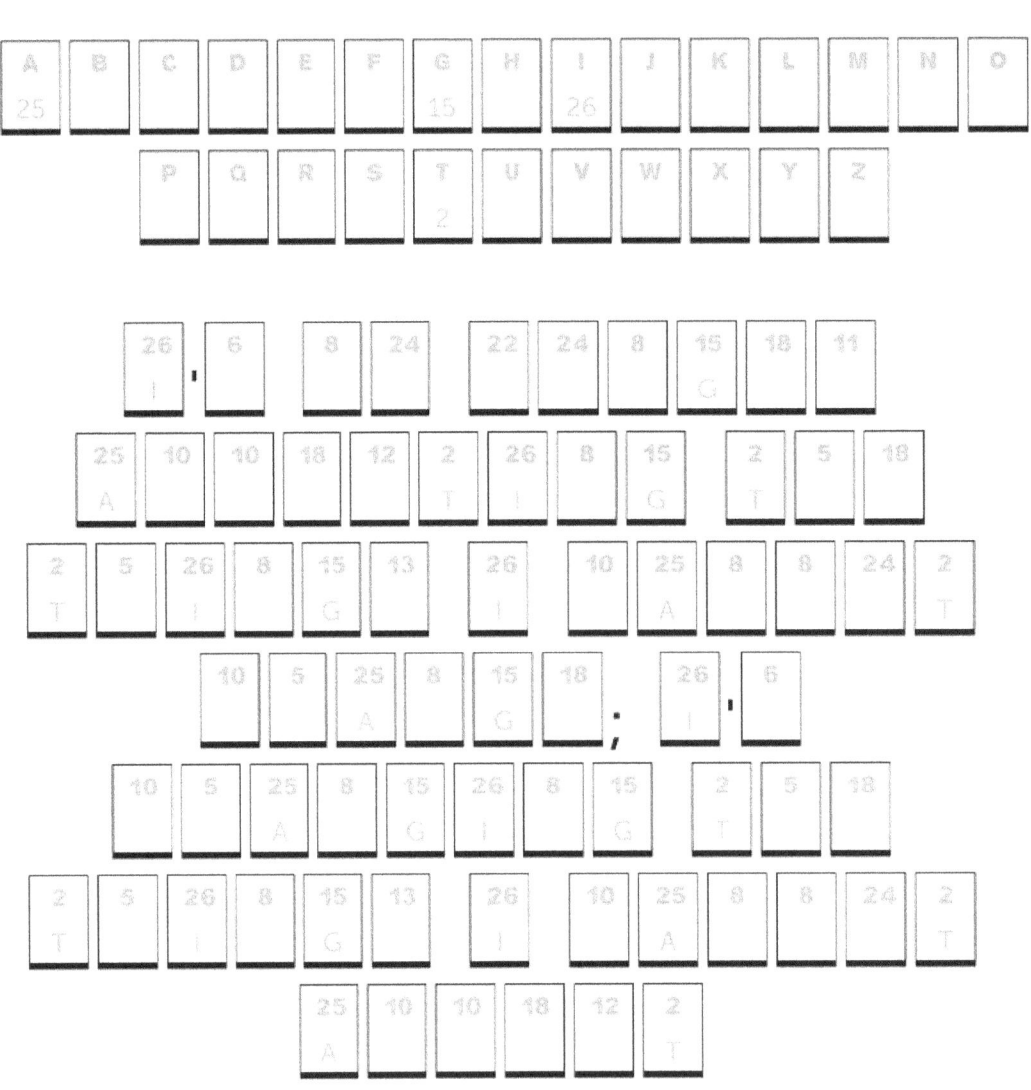

August 30, 1948 – December 4, 1969
ABOLITIONIST

75

LEFT BLANK ON PURPOSE

Fred Hampton

Fred Hampton

Fred Hampton

Fred Hampton

Fred Hampton

Fred Hampton

Directions: read the bio below and answer the following questions.

Hi, my name is Fredrick Allen Hampton Sr. I was born on August 30, 1948, in Summit Argo, IL. I graduated from Proviso East High School. I went to Triton Junior College, where I majored in pre-law. I planned to become more familiar with the legal system to use it as a defense against police when fellow Black Panthers followed police as part of our community supervision program to watch out for police brutality. I used my knowledge of the law as a defense. I was a member of the National Association for the Advancement of Colored People (NAACP), the Black Panther Party (BPP) and the Student Nonviolent Coordinating Committee (SNCC). As the chairman of Illinois' BPP, I formed an alliance between the Panthers, the Lords and the white working-class Young Patriots so that we could fight poverty and the lack of resources in our communities. The alliance was known as the Rainbow Coalition and helped establish a progressive, fundamentally socialist movement.

1. What did I study in college?
   A. Medicine
   B. Business
   C. Pre-Law
2. What association was I the chairman of?
   A. NAACP
   B. BPP
   C. SNCC
3. What is the name of the alliance I created?
   A. Rainbow Coalition
   B. Treaty of Alliance
   C. Alliance for Progress

Directions: Find the words associated with Fred's life and career.

```
R B R R N R T E L T X G B N U I I R
P L Y P N O I T A N I S S A S S A C
G A T S X N G N T N K K N T M D W U
G C B T G O C H I C A G O B U P P V
F K G O Z I K V I Y G T F L B U I O
V P D I X T F B V R O S O X V T C E
E A I R I Q O S A Q I K I Q U Y X
G N L T D L S R T N J V D E O U P Y
S T K A A J P E O U I B F V C A O
R H S P K O L L T I M T B Y A J X U
D E O G S C S E H T X C R A Q Q Q N
R R C N M W Y T D U Y A N S C O N G
U P D U A O U N X L T C K T X Q M L
Y A D O H B T I V O Z P K P A Q P O
Y R R Y W N K O C V F T K W U R Y R
Z T S A M I U C H E B E Y W X H G D
J Y D D G A H Z Y R Z G S D C Y N S
N A A G P R M B L G R K Z R W J W X
```

Find These Words

ACTIVIST   REVOLUTIONARY   BLACKPANTHERPARTY
RAINBOWCOALITION CHICAGO   NAACP
ASSASSINATION   COINTELPRO   YOUNGPATRIOTS
YOUNGLORDS

Directions: Read and answer the questions. 14th Amendment facts. Use the internet to help you.

1) What group did the Fourteenth Amendment say the Bill of Rights applied to?

State governments

Foreign governments

The British

2) What group of people did the amendment say could not hold public office?

Former slave owners

Former slaves

People that participated in a rebellion

3) The Fourteenth Amendment was initially put into place to protect what group of people?

Former slave owners

Freed slaves

Members of Congress

4) The 14th Amendment guarantees citizenship if which one of the following is true?

You were born in the U.S.

You have lived in the U.S. for ten years.

You have family members that are U.S. citizens.

5) The 14th Amendment was ratified in 1868. What does ratified mean?

Written

Signed into law

Changed

6) Prior to the amendment, how were former slaves counted when determining the number of representatives, a state would have?

one fourth

one half

three fifths

Directions: Read and answer the questions below. There are clues in the puzzle to help you. Try and solve the cryptic message.

Clue for cryptic message: Fred was considered to be this.

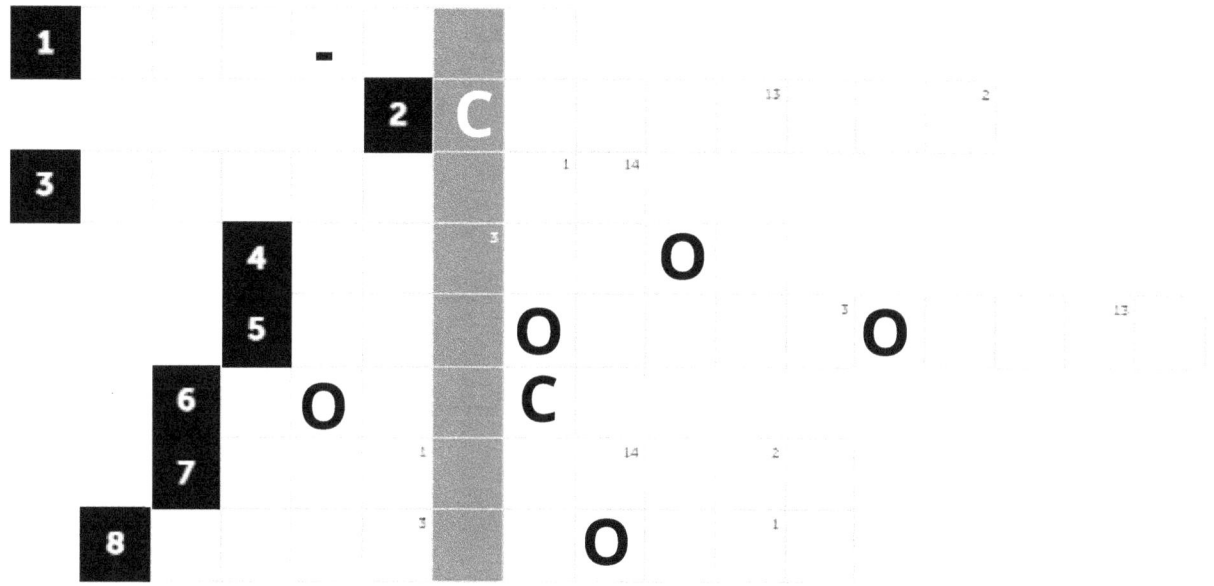

Questions

1) Fred study _____ at Triton Junior College.
2) Fred was the deputy _____ of the national Black Panther Party.
3) Fred was _____ by the FBI as part of its COINTELPRO program.
4) Fred formed an alliance known as the _____ Coalition.
5) Fred mantra was I am a _____.
6) Fred was killed by Chicago _____ officers in a raid that was never justified.
7) Fred served as an NAACP Youth Council _____.
8) Fred _____ the governors of his school to hire more black staff.

Directions: This is the WGLT Challenge. Solve the cryptogram. As the puzzle solver, you need to find which number belongs to which character. And this can be pretty challenging! You will need to match the number with the letter. There are some letters given to you below. This will help you solve the other words and unlock more characters. **Good Luck.**

82

Jesse Jackson

Jesse Jackson

October 8, 1941 - PRESENT
POLITICAL ACTIVIST/BAPTIST MINISTER

83

Jesse Jackson

Jesse Jackson

Jesse Jackson

Jesse Jackson

Jesse Jackson

Jesse Jackson

Directions: read the bio below and answer the following questions.

Hi, my name is Jesse Jackson. I was born on October 8, 1941, in Greenville, SC. I graduated from Sterling High School in Greenville, where I was elected student class president, finished tenth in my class and earned letters in baseball, football and basketball. In 1959, I was given a football scholarship to the University of Illinois, but I transferred to NC AGT University. I graduated with a bachelor's degree in sociology. In 1965, I participated in the Selma to Montgomery marches. Martin Luther King, Jr. gave me a role in the Southern Christian Leadership Conference (SCLC). In 1968, I became an ordained minister. In 1983, I announced my campaign for president of the United States in the 1984 election and I became the second African American to mount a nationwide campaign for president as a Democrat. I helped organize the Rainbow Coalition and People United to Save Humanity (PUSH).

1. What college did I graduate from?
   A. University of Illinois
   B. Fisk University
   C. NC A&T University
2. What sport did I get a scholarship for?
   A. Baseball
   B. Basketball
   C. Football
3. What organization didn't I create?
   A. Rainbow Coalition
   B. SCLC
   C. PUSH

Directions: Answer the questions, to solve the crossword puzzle. You can use the internet if you get stuck on any question.

Across

1) Jesse received a _____ to play college football at the University of Illinois.
4) Jesse was a candidate for the Democratic _____ nomination in 1984.
6) Jesse _____ the National Rainbow Coalition in 1986.
7) Jesse was the national _____ of Operation Breadbasket.
8) Jesse participated in the _____ to Montgomery marches.

Down

2) Ebony Magazine named Jesse to its "100 most _____ black Americans" list in 1971.
3) Jesse was awarded the Presidential Medal of _____.
5) Jesse attended the University of _____ before transferring to North Carolina A&T.

Directions: Read and answer the questions. Electoral votes per state. Use the internet to help you. Answers will depend on your state.

The presidential election decides who will be the president and vice president for the next four years. The winner of the election is determined by electoral votes. The number of electoral votes each state has is determined by the number of people living in the state. In every state except Maine and Nebraska, if a candidate wins the vote, they win all the electoral votes for that state. A candidate with more than half of the electoral votes wins the presidential election.

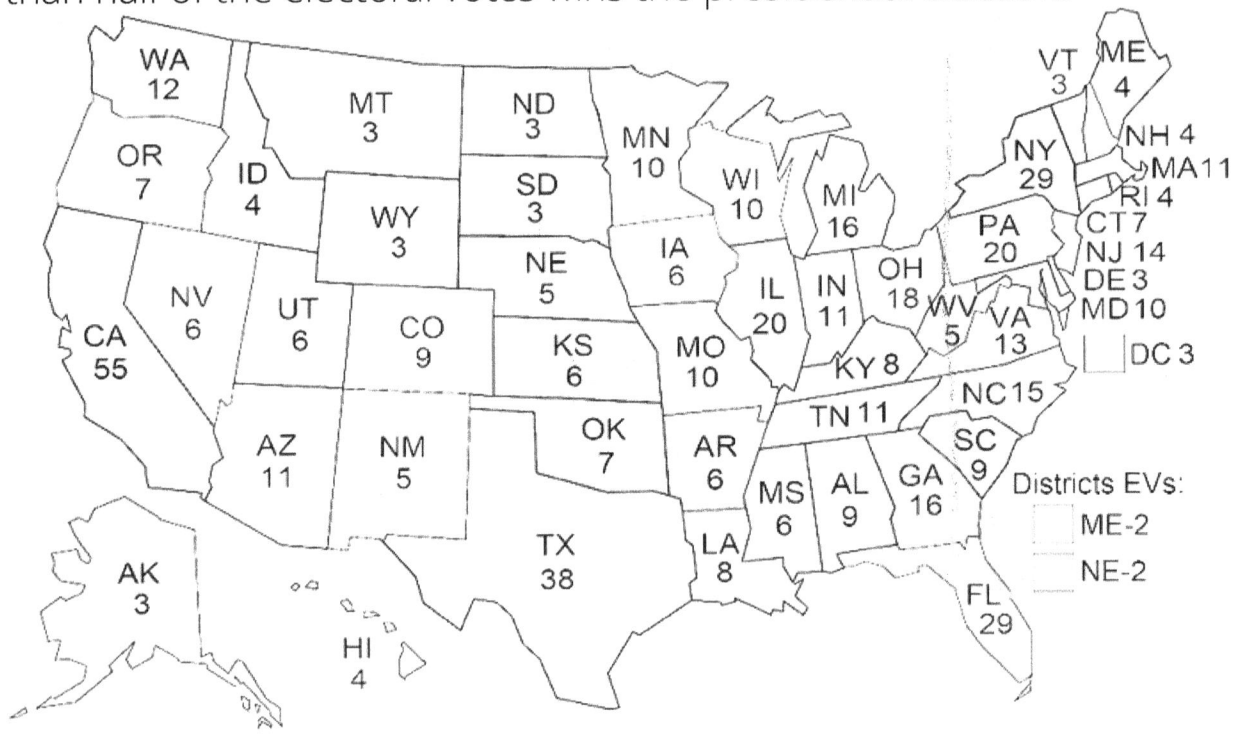

1) How many electoral votes does your state have.

2) Is your state considered a Republican or Democratic or a toss-up state.

3) Who is your favorite President and why?

88

Directions: Unscramble the words below about Jesse. See if you can get the bonus word.

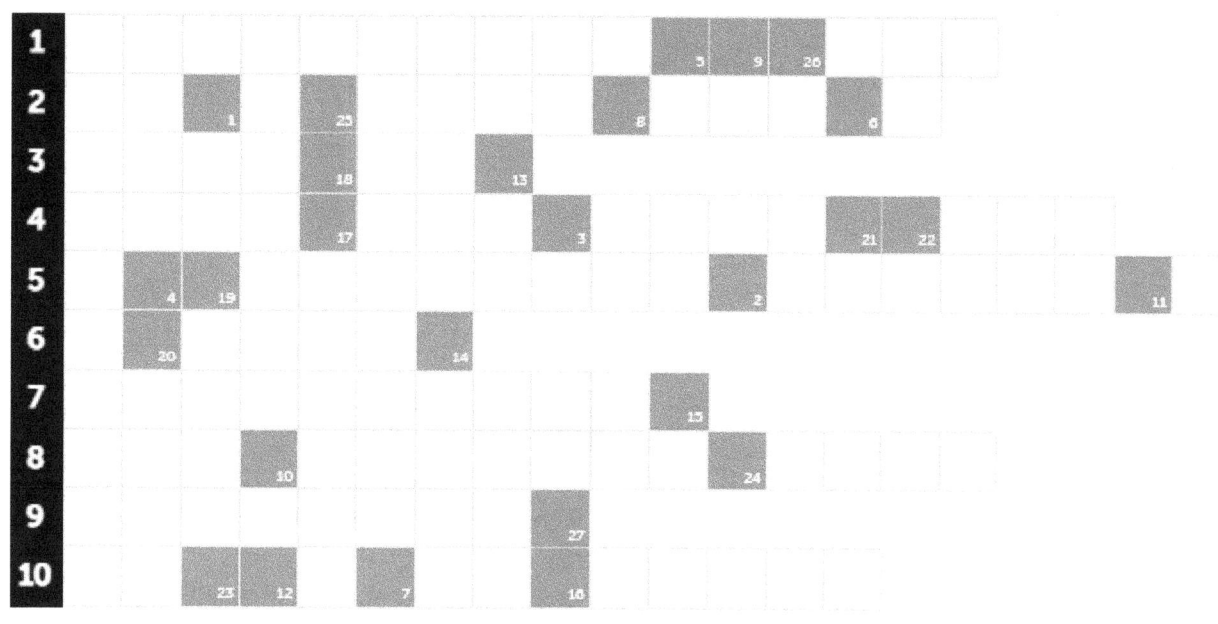

BONUS WORD

Unscramble Words

1) inoaiionltcawbro **2)** siaittmibpstner **3)** tsaivict
4) itmfliroaotcusicdb **5)** dobntarotbepkeeaasir **6)** hacicgo
7) hivigcirlts **8)** c&olatahinraornt **9)** ysooclgoi
10) shtosdrnaeuoas

Directions: This is the WGLT Challenge. Solve the cryptogram. As the puzzle solver, you need to find which number belongs to which character. And this can be pretty challenging! You will need to match the number with the letter. There are some letters given to you below. This will help you solve the other words and unlock more characters. **Good Luck.**

Dorothy Height

Dorothy Height

March 24, 1912 – April 20, 2010
CIVIL RIGHTS/WOMEN RIGHTS ACTIVIST

LEFT BLANK ON PURPOSE

Dorothy Height

Dorothy Height

Dorothy Height

Dorothy Height

Dorothy Height

Dorothy Height

Directions: read the bio below and answer the following questions.

Hi, my name is Dorothy Height. I was born on March 24, 1912, in Richmond, VA. I graduated from Rankin High School in 1929. I was accepted to Barnard College in 1929 but was denied entrance because the school had an unwritten policy of admitting only two Black students per year. I went to New York University instead and earned an undergraduate degree in 1932 and a master's degree in educational psychology the following year. I was also a member of the Delta Sigma Theta sorority and served as the national president of the sorority from 1947 to 1956. I became the president of the National Council of Negro Women (NCNW) in 1958 and remained in that position until 1990. One of the things that I was known for was focusing on the issues of African American women, which included unemployment, illiteracy and voter awareness. I was the first leader in the civil rights movement to recognize inequality for women and African Americans as problems that should be considered as a whole.

1. **What is my Master's Degree in?**
   A. **Politics**
   B. **Criminal Justice**
   C. **Educational Psychology**
2. **What year did I become the president of NCNW?**
   A. **1990**
   B. **1958**
   C. **1947**
3. **What sorority am I apart of?**
   A. **Alpha Kapa Alpha**
   B. **Sigma Gamma Rho**
   C. **Delta Sigma Theta**

Directions: Find the words associated with Dorothy's life and career.

```
B E L M O N T R E P O R T N W W A L
A L U L D M Q J Z Q I Z I Q O N S Y
S G Y I N C Z F H D O I D M I L B P
Y D Z M M H W L C N H L E H N W R X
V P V G L Q S K R M A N U X R E G Y
T N L X B Y Q T N T S I C X S S E S
C A J E P X Y A L R X E T I S W E E
I S F E M E D M I W Z Q D S L I S Y
M A M T J U B G E N I E K N I T R O
R I X Y S K H O M M N U P G T R F N
Q B A M H T J E Y T P H J R U D H U
O M X V S G U Y G O L O H C Y S P C
L U G S S T H G I R L I V I C Q K P
Z L C A T E H T A M G I S A T L E D
N O W R G Y J A Y D F D Y D U F Z A
W C D D C X I S G I B N C G R F K E
M A R C H O N W A S H I N G T O N A
U F O S L H K V L U W W Q P I G W L
```

Find These Words

PRESIDENT   CHRISTIAN   CIVILRIGHTS
WOMENSRIGHTS   PSYCHOLOGY   DELTASIGMATHETA
BIGSIX   MARCHONWASHINGTON   COLUMBIA
BELMONTREPORT

Directions: Read and answer the questions. Describe Dorothy using five adjectives. Then use that adjective in a sentence.

1) _____

_____

2) _____

_____

3) _____

_____

4) _____

_____

5) _____

_____

Directions: Read and answer the questions below. There are clues in the puzzle to help you. Try and solve the cryptic message.

Clue for cryptic message: Dorothy was this a lot.

Questions

1) Dorothy had a master's degree in _____.

2) Dorothy was _____ of the Leadership Conference's Executive Committee.

3) Dorothy was the president of the National Council of Negro _____ for 40 years.

4) Dorothy helped found the National Women's Political _____ with Gloria Steinem, Betty Friedan and Shirley Chisholm.

5) Dorothy was an active member of Delta _____ Theta sorority.

6) Dorothy was a founding member of the Council for United Civil Rights _____ (CUCRL).

7) President Barack Obama called Dorothy "the godmother of the civil rights _____.

8) Dorothy was the president to the Young Women's _____ Association (YWCA).

9) Dorothy received the _____ Medal of Freedom.

Directions: This is the WGLT Challenge. Solve the cryptogram. As the puzzle solver, you need to find which number belongs to which character. And this can be pretty challenging! You will need to match the number with the letter. There are some letters given to you below. This will help you solve the other words and unlock more characters. **Good Luck.**

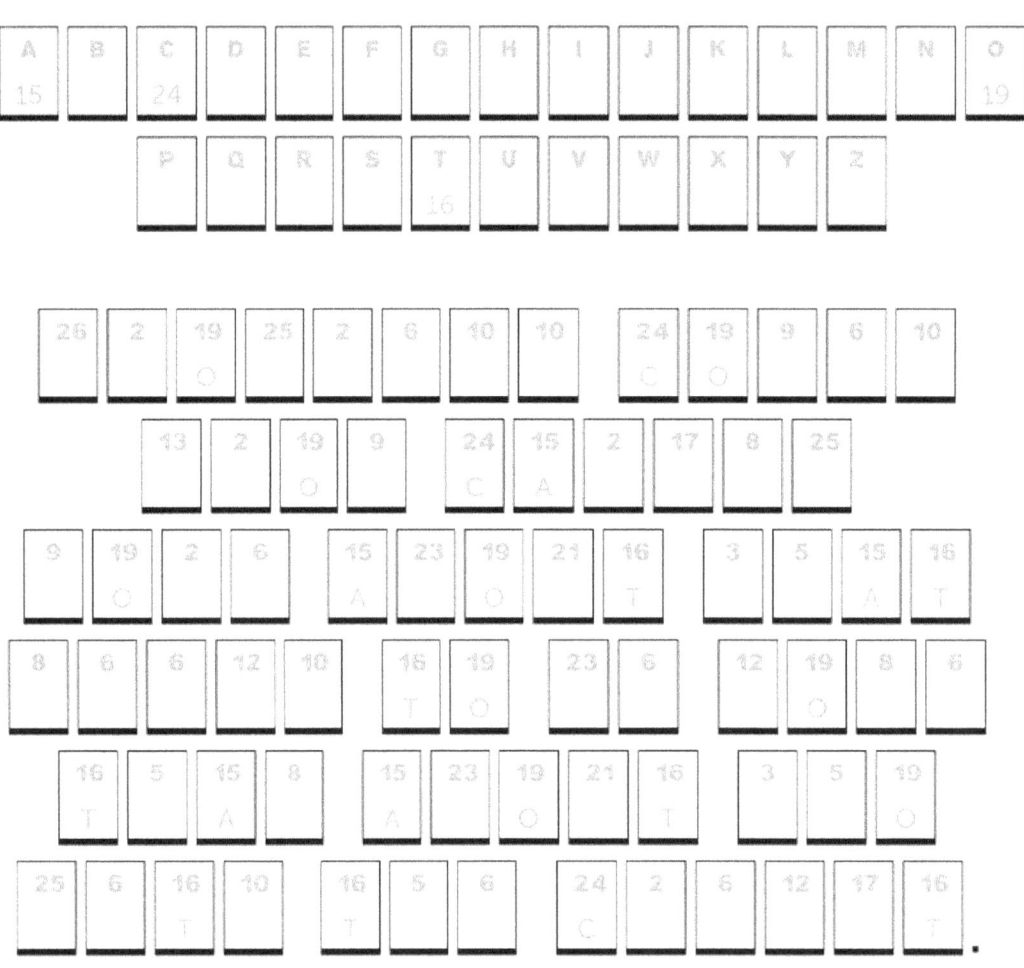

May 19, 1925 – February 21, 1965
MUSLIM MINISTER/HUMAN RIGHTS ACTIVIST

Malcolm X

Malcolm X

Malcolm X

Malcolm X

Malcolm X

Malcolm X

Directions: read the bio below and answer the following questions.

Hi, my name is Malcolm Little. I was born on May 19, 1925, in Omaha, NV. In 1941, I attended Mason High School but dropped out after a white teacher told me that practicing law was "no realistic goal." In 1946, I was arrested and began serving an eight-to-ten-year sentence at Charlestown State Prison for larceny and breaking and entering. In late 1948, I wrote to Elijah Muhammad, who was the leader of the Nation of Islam. He advised me to renounce my past, humbly bow in prayer to God and promise never to engage in destructive behavior again. I soon became a member of the Nation of Islam. In 1950, the FBI opened a file on me after I wrote a letter from prison to President Truman that expressed my opposition to the Korean War and declared myself to be a communist. After I was granted parole in August 1952, I became the assistant minister of the Nation's Temple Number One in Detroit. I later established Temple 11 and Temple 12. In 1954, I was selected to lead Temple 7 in Harlem. By that time, I was under surveillance by the FBI for possible communist associations and my rapid ascent in the Nation of Islam.

1. What did I go to prison for?
   A. Larceny
   B. Murder
   C. Kidnapping
2. What year did I become a member of Nation of Islam?
   A. 1946
   B. 1948
   C. 1950
3. What Temple was I selected to lead?
   A. Temple Number 1
   B. Temple Number 11
   C. Temple Number 7

Directions: Answer the questions, to solve the crossword puzzle. You can use the internet if you get stuck on any question.

Across
1) Malcolm penned a letter to President _____ declaring himself a communist who opposed the Korean War.
5) Malcolm's eighth-grade teacher discouraged him from pursuing his interest in becoming a _____.
6) Malcolm turned to the Nation of Islam while in _____.
7) Harvard and Oxford, invited Malcolm to speak and _____.
8) Malcolm's pilgrimage to Mecca _____ his political views.

Down
2) Malcolm founded the newspaper, _____ Speaks.
3) Malcolm's nickname was "_____" because of the color of hair.
4) Malcolm was named _____ of the prestigious Temple 7 in Harlem.

Directions: Read and answer the questions. Nation of Islam. Use the internet to help you.

1) What is it called when Muslims don't eat or drink from dawn to sunset during Ramadan?

Salat

Zakat

Fasting

2) What are the five basic acts that form the framework of the religion of Islam?

Five Holy Books

Five Pillars of Islam

Five Commandments

3) What is a Hadith?

A text describing the actions and sayings of Muhammad

A Muslim holy city

An Islamic religious leader

4) What are people who believe and follow the religion of Islam called?

Middle Easterners

Muslims

Arabs

5) What does the Arabic word 'Islam' mean?

Submission

Worship

Peace

6) What direction do Muslim's face when praying?

North

Towards the city of Mecca

They don't face any specific direction

7) What is the Quran?

The most holy city of Islam

The leader of the Muslim world

The holy book of Islam

Directions: Unscramble the words below about Malcolm. See if you can get the bonus word.

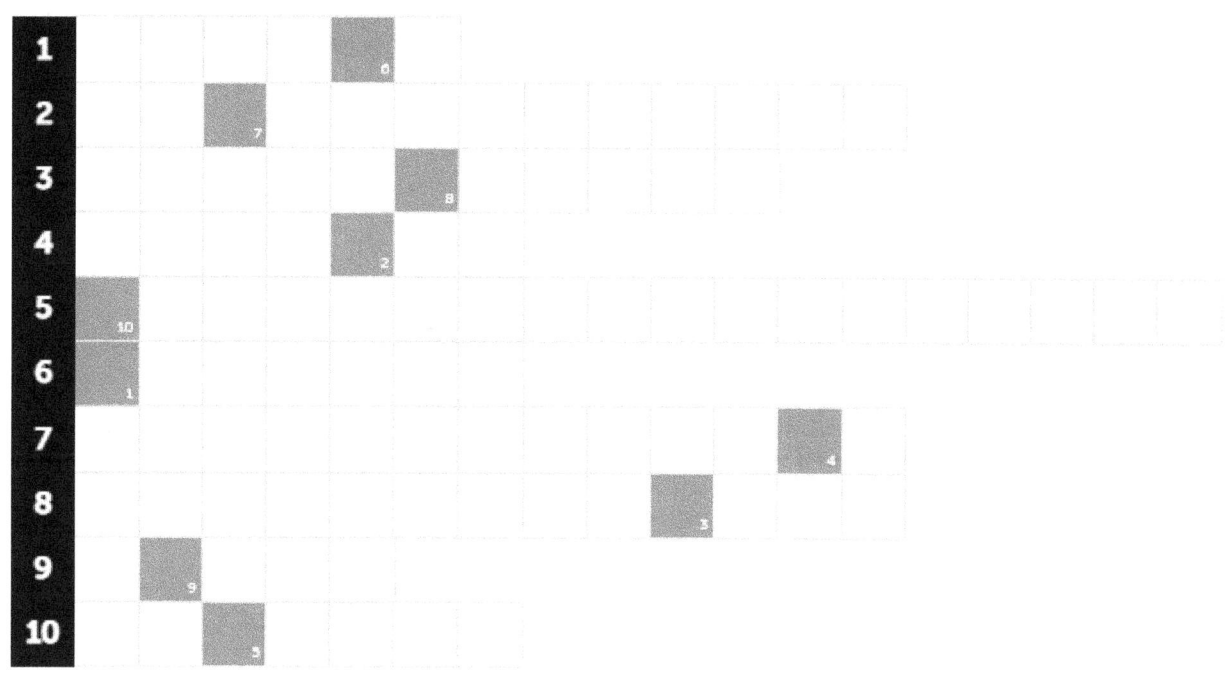

BONUS WORD

| 1 | 2 | 3 | 4 | 5 | 6 | 7 | 8 | 9 | 10 |

Unscramble Words

1) mslimu
2) liinsfamnoota
3) clrhtiviisg
4) yenclra
5) hninestnieedacmsrf
6) dierott
7) elenumm7etprb
8) iiaanstssoasn
9) amcce
10) amowlOe

105

Directions: This is the WGLT Challenge. Solve the cryptogram. As the puzzle solver, you need to find which number belongs to which character. And this can be pretty challenging! You will need to match the number with the letter. There are some letters given to you below. This will help you solve the other words and unlock more characters. **Good Luck.**

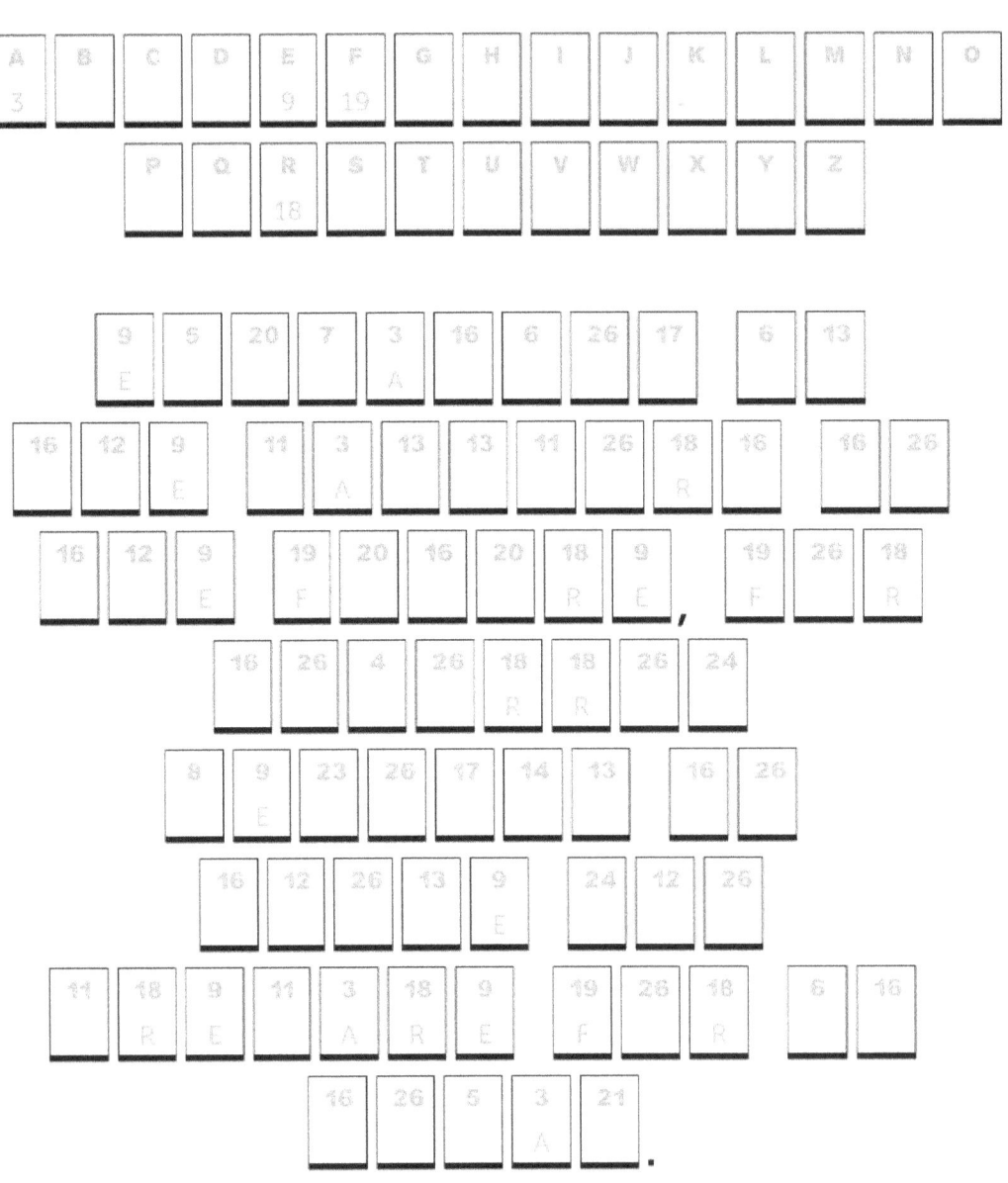

106

Kamala Harris

Kamala Harris

OCTOBER 20, 1964 - PRESENT
VICE PRESIDENT

LEFT BLANK ON PURPOSE

Kamala Harris

Kamala Harris

Kamala Harris

Kamala Harris

Kamala Harris

Kamala Harris

Directions: read the bio below and answer the following questions.

Hi, my name is Kamala D. Harris. I was born on October 20, 1964, in Oakland, CA. I graduated from Westmount High School. I received my bachelor's degree in political science and economics from Howard University. I also became a member of the Alpha Kappa Alpha sorority. In 1989, I received my Juris Doctor degree from the University of California and was admitted to the California Bar in June 1990. That same year, I was hired as a deputy district attorney in Alameda County, CA. In 2002, I became the first person of color to be elected as a district attorney of San Francisco. In 2011, I became the first woman, the first African American and the first South Asian American to hold the office of Attorney General in California's history. In 2016, I won the CA Senate seat. On January 20, 2021, I became the United States' first female vice president, the highest-ranking female elected official in U.S. history and the first African American and first Asian American vice president.

1. What Sorority am I a member of?
    A. Zeta Phi Beta
    B. Alpha Kappa Alpha
    C. Delta Sigma Theta
2. What college did I get my Juris Doctor from?
    A. Howard University
    B. Berkley University
    C. University of California
3. I was the first women in U.S. history receive this title?
    A. President
    B. Vice President
    C. Sectary of Defense

Directions: Find the words associated with Kamala's life and career.

```
C Y A D H Y N A N W Y H N M Q G N I
D O O N P M D N A I C I T I L O P A
I H G D J A I P F E F Y T V L I N Q
S U Z J L T X E F R L X U D A N B B
T L Y W K K P A U T H O R C I R A C
R H O W A R D U N I V E R S I T Y O
I V M V O K G M Z N I K L N C A S L
C K O Z N L O T T O L J L K O P I P
A L Z Q I F S Y T I R O R O S A K A
T F O L T L Q M P X K I E Q T W W C
T R V I C E P R E S I D E N T U U Y
O Y R W E O I B U Z E N C X A W S G
R O G V L S E N A T O R B H L E A Y
N F H D U Q Q C K V H G G O A P X X
E C O U D C C A Q A F X E F M L D G
Y W A W H O A P I M M L R X O G F E
W V M H Y X A F C W Y F Z L M R T L
Y R M L R O T U C E S O R P F A B M
```

Find These Words

HOWARDUNIVERSITY SENATOR VICEPRESIDENT
POLITICIAN PROSECUTOR AKASORORITY
AUTHOR MOMALA LOTUS
DISTRICATTORNEY

Directions: Read and answer the questions. Presidential and Vice President responsibilities. Use the internet to help you.

1) True or False: Each cabinet member must be approved by the U.S. Congress.

TRUE

FALSE

2) Which part of the Executive Branch votes to break a tie in the Senate?

Vice President

Secretary of State

White House Head of Staff

3) How many different Cabinet departments are there?

15

10

27

4) What is the main job of the Vice President?

To lead the cabinet meetings and take notes for the president.

To take over as president if the president dies or can no longer do the job of president.

The vice president acts as Commander and Chief of the U.S. armed forces.

5) Which of the following is not a power of the president?

The power to sign treaties with foreign nations.

The power to veto legislation from congress.

The power to break a tie vote in the Senate.

6) Which of the following is not a part of the Executive Branch?

The Vice President

The Supreme Court

The Secretary of State

7) What are some of the functions of the Executive Office of the President?

Brief the press on the president's activities.

Advise the president on national security issues.

Assist the president in running the many responsibilities of the Executive Branch.

All of the above.

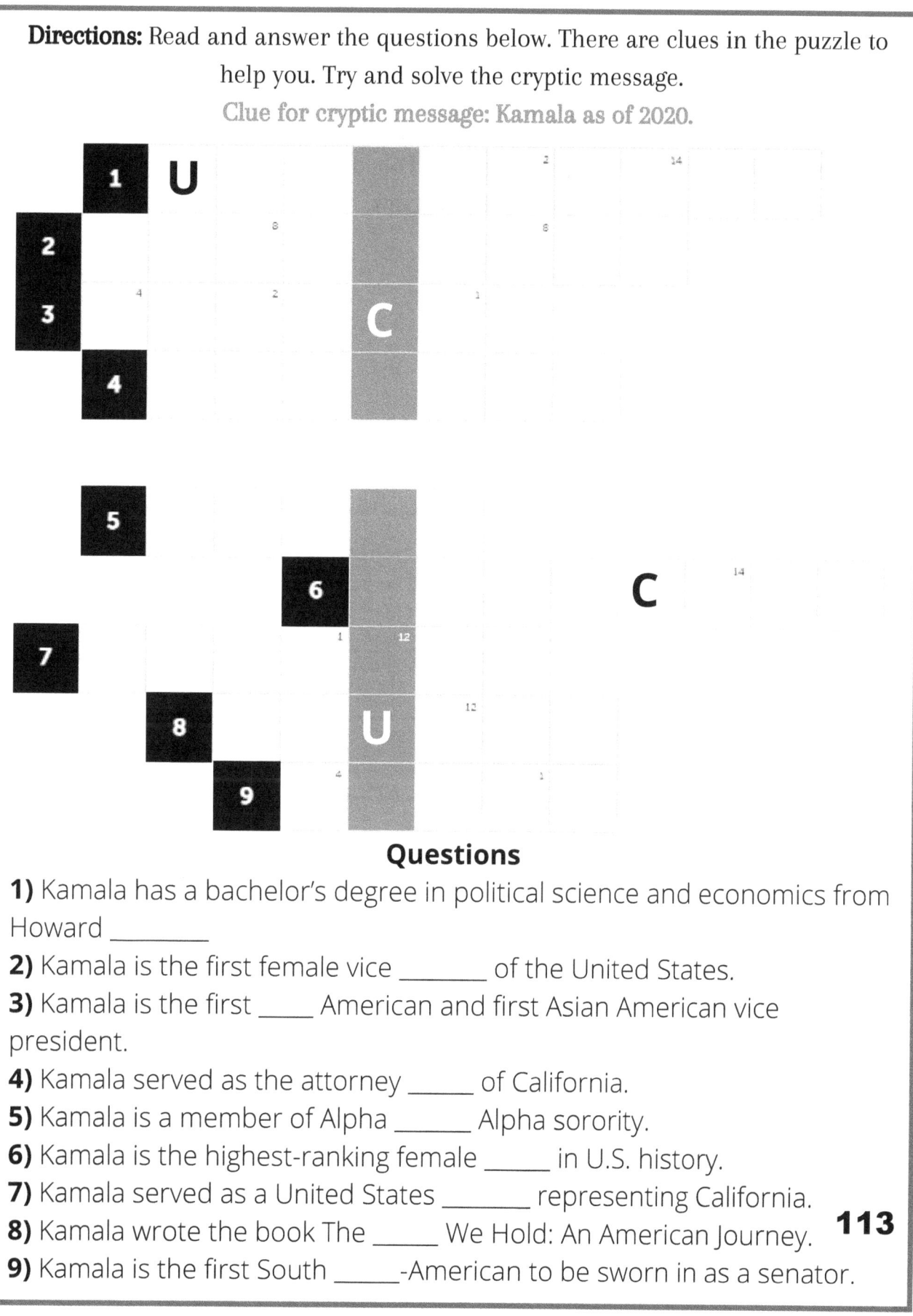

Directions: Read and answer the questions below. There are clues in the puzzle to help you. Try and solve the cryptic message.

Clue for cryptic message: Kamala as of 2020.

Questions

1) Kamala has a bachelor's degree in political science and economics from Howard _____
2) Kamala is the first female vice _____ of the United States.
3) Kamala is the first ____ American and first Asian American vice president.
4) Kamala served as the attorney _____ of California.
5) Kamala is a member of Alpha _____ Alpha sorority.
6) Kamala is the highest-ranking female _____ in U.S. history.
7) Kamala served as a United States _____ representing California.
8) Kamala wrote the book The _____ We Hold: An American Journey.
9) Kamala is the first South _____-American to be sworn in as a senator.

Directions: This is the WGLT Challenge. Solve the cryptogram. As the puzzle solver, you need to find which number belongs to which character. And this can be pretty challenging! You will need to match the number with the letter. There are some letters given to you below. This will help you solve the other words and unlock more characters. **Good Luck.**

Medgar Evers

Medgar Evers

115

July 2, 1925 – June 12, 1963
CIVIL RIGHTS ACTIVIST

LEFT BLANK ON PURPOSE

Medgar Evers

Medgar Evers

Medgar Evers

Medgar Evers

Medgar Evers

Medgar Evers

Directions: read the bio below and answer the following questions.

Hi, my name is Medgar Evers. I was born on July 2, 1925, in Decatur, MS. I attended all-Black schools in the dual and segregated public educational system of Newton County. After I graduated, I served in the U.S. Army during World War II from 1943 to 1945. I fought in the Battle of Normandy in 1944. I was honorably discharged as a sergeant. In 1948, I enrolled at Alcorn Agricultural and Mechanical College (which is an HBCU and is now Alcorn State University) and earned my Bachelor of Arts in 1952. On November 24, 1954, I was named as the NAACP's first field secretary for Mississippi. In this position, I helped organize boycotts and set up new local chapters of the NAACP. I was involved with James Meredith's efforts to enroll in the University of Mississippi in the early 1960s and after the Supreme Court ruled in our favor in 1962, Meredith was successfully admitted and graduated the following year (since he had previously earned credits at another school). The University of Mississippi (Ole Miss) was integrated and received nationwide attention because of that.

1. What Branch of Service did I serve in?
    A. U.S. Marine Corps
    B. U.S. Army
    C. U.S. Navy
2. What HBCU did I go to?
    A. Alcorn State University
    B. Alabama State University
    C. Southern University
3. What college did I help integrate?
    A. Ole Miss
    B. Mississippi State University
    C. Alcorn State University

Directions: Answer the questions, to solve the crossword puzzle. You can use the internet if you get stuck on any question.

Across

1) In 1994, Medgar's _____ was finally brought to justice thirty-one years after his death.

3) Medgar was buried in _____ Cemetery with full military honors.

7) Medgar earned his _____ of Arts from Alcorn College now Alcorn State University.

8) Medgar was _____ the murder of Emmett Till.

Down

2) Medgar was the NAACP's first field _____ in the South.

4) Medgar participated in the _____ invasion.

5) Medgar was a _____ in the United States Army.

6) Medgar was a World War II _____.

Directions: Read and answer the questions. Government for the State. Use the internet to help you.

1) What is the main way that states and local governments get money to run the government?

Parking and speeding ticket fines

Taxes

Tariffs on imports

2) Which branch of government has the Supreme Court and lower courts to try cases?

The Executive

The Judicial

The County

3) Which of the following is typically not a member of the executive branch of state government?

Governor

Secretary of State

Chief Justice

4) When you buy something at the store, a tax is added in that goes to the local government. What is this tax called?

Store tax

Sales tax

Property tax

5) What is the tax called that you pay each year when you own a piece of land or a home?

Income tax

Property tax

Sales tax

6) Who is the leader of the state government?

The Secretary of State

The mayor

The governor

Directions: Unscramble the words below about Medgar. See if you can get the bonus word.

BONUS WORD

Unscramble Words

1) vsicriigtlh
2) cpnaa
3) myrusa
4) onontleniv
5) rrdo2wlwa
6) igrtvoigshnt
7) eeatnrcobtmav
8) vacmsiit
9) gtseearn
10) tonseftrnerw

Directions: This is the WGLT Challenge. Solve the cryptogram. As the puzzle solver, you need to find which number belongs to which character. And this can be pretty challenging! You will need to match the number with the letter. There are some letters given to you below. This will help you solve the other words and unlock more characters. **Good Luck.**

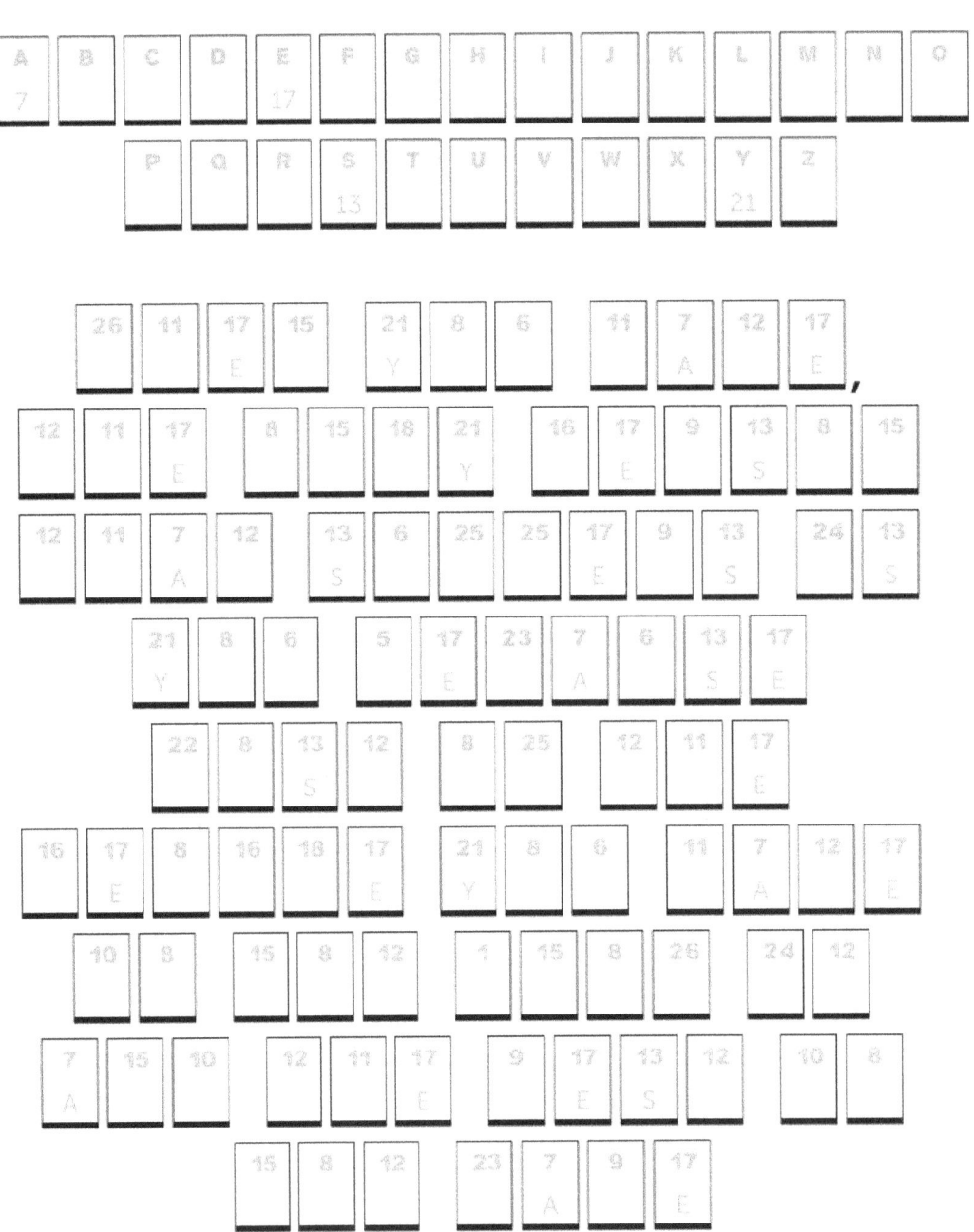

Colin Kaepernick

Colin Kaepernick

November 3, 1987 - PRESENT
CIVIL RIGHTS ACTIVIST

123

LEFT BLANK ON PURPOSE

Colin Kaepernick

Colin Kaepernick

Colin Kaepernick

Colin Kaepernick

Colin Kaepernick

Colin Kaepernick

Directions: read the bio below and answer the following questions.

Hi, my name is Colin Kaepernick. I was born on November 3, 1987, in Milwaukee, WI. I graduated from John H. Pitman High School. I graduated from the University of Nevada with a bachelor's degree in business management. I was drafted by the 49ers in 2011. I was an off-and-on starter for the 49ers. In 2016, I sat during the playing of the U.S. national anthem before the game rather than standing, which is customary, as a protest against racial injustice, police brutality and oppression in the country. The following week and throughout the regular season, I kneeled during the anthem. The protests received highly polarized reactions. Some people praised me and my stand against racism and others denounced my protests. In 2016, my partner Nessa and I founded the "Know Your Rights Camp," which is an organization that hosts free seminars for disadvantaged youths to teach them about self-empowerment, American history and legal rights.

1. What college did I get my degree from?
   A. UCLA
   B. University of Wisconsin
   C. University of Nevada
2. What year did I get drafted to the 49ers?
   A. 2011
   B. 2009
   C. 2012
3. What organization did I help found?
   A. NAACP
   B. Know Your Rights Camp
   C. National Urban League

Directions: Find the words associated with Colin's life and career.

Y	F	E	Q	I	Q	N	H	F	L	H	H	S	J	Y	Y	Q	F
R	P	O	R	7	K	C	I	N	R	E	P	E	A	K	J	X	N
M	P	J	L	Z	Y	J	Y	B	S	P	Z	T	B	G	O	O	E
A	P	G	N	A	C	C	I	K	T	G	T	H	N	Y	B	V	
Y	S	U	A	A	X	S	B	U	C	O	G	A	C	I	H	C	A
E	F	W	M	W	F	H	B	K	E	C	J	P	O	U	H	E	D
J	N	G	V	C	W	Z	L	O	E	S	I	Y	A	S	T	N	A
X	I	T	O	I	Q	W	X	N	G	T	Z	M	N	R	Y	K	W
W	I	O	G	V	B	K	J	B	C	A	K	M	T	E	A	G	O
I	R	F	I	I	W	T	W	H	S	W	D	L	M	N	G	V	L
Y	H	P	O	L	I	C	E	B	R	U	T	A	L	I	T	Y	F
C	X	I	K	R	K	R	A	V	A	O	F	W	P	N	H	G	P
G	P	O	E	I	G	L	Q	Z	Q	S	D	U	H	Y	H	U	A
W	C	M	W	G	D	E	L	E	E	N	K	U	A	T	U	K	C
Z	S	B	Z	H	P	N	H	X	U	V	H	C	G	R	K	V	K
Q	U	A	R	T	E	R	B	A	C	K	P	P	E	O	F	Y	S
A	K	T	L	S	B	I	T	Q	A	P	L	R	Q	F	D	Q	G
Z	W	M	E	H	T	N	A	L	A	N	O	I	T	A	N	U	H

Find These Words

NATIONALANTHEM   PITCHER   FORTYNINERS
CIVILRIGHTS   POLICEBRUTALITY   QUARTERBACK
NEVADAWOLFPACK   CHICAGOCUBS   KAEPERNICK7
KNEELED

Directions: Read and answer the questions. Bill of rights. Use the internet to help you.

1) True or False: The ninth amendment states that 100% of the rights of the citizens are called out in the Constitution. That they have no rights beyond what the Constitution says.

TRUE

FALSE

2) Which of the following describes the Bill of Rights?

A document that insures the basic freedoms of the citizens of the United States.

A document that protects the freedom of religion and speech.

All of the above.

3) Who wrote the amendments that became the Bill of Rights?

James Madison

George Washington

John Adams

4) Which amendment guarantees citizens the freedom of religion and the freedom of speech?

The fifth

The second

The first

5) What historic document is the Bill of Rights a part of?

The Pledge of Allegiance

The Constitution

The Emancipation Proclamation

6) What right does the fifth amendment protect?

The right to choose not to testify against oneself

The right to bear arms

Freedom of speech

7) How many amendments are included in the Bill of Rights?

3

The first 10

5

Directions: Read and answer the questions below. There are clues in the puzzle to help you. Try and solve the cryptic message.

Clue for cryptic message: Colin was this in the end.

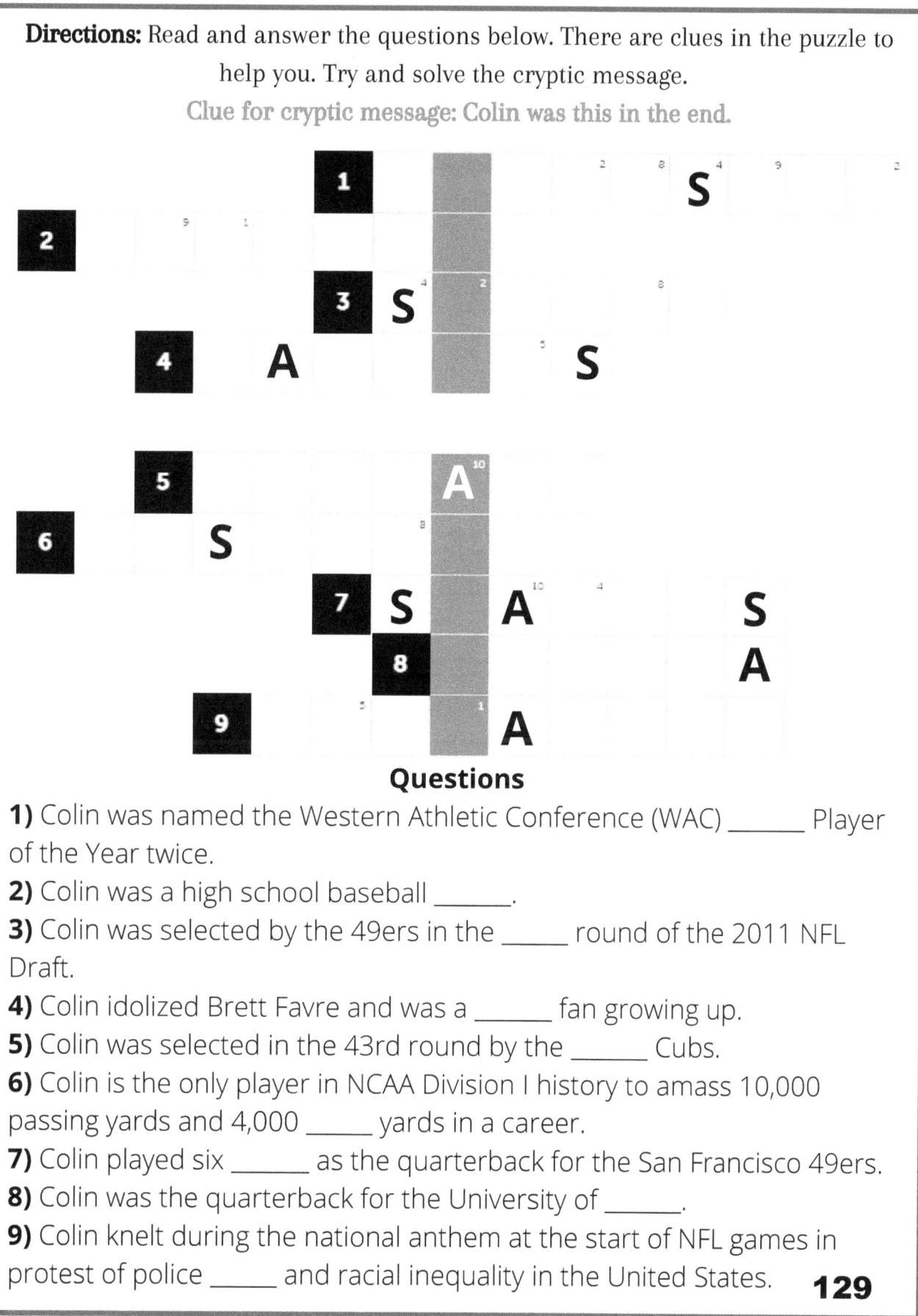

Questions

1) Colin was named the Western Athletic Conference (WAC) _____ Player of the Year twice.
2) Colin was a high school baseball _____.
3) Colin was selected by the 49ers in the _____ round of the 2011 NFL Draft.
4) Colin idolized Brett Favre and was a _____ fan growing up.
5) Colin was selected in the 43rd round by the _____ Cubs.
6) Colin is the only player in NCAA Division I history to amass 10,000 passing yards and 4,000 _____ yards in a career.
7) Colin played six _____ as the quarterback for the San Francisco 49ers.
8) Colin was the quarterback for the University of _____.
9) Colin knelt during the national anthem at the start of NFL games in protest of police _____ and racial inequality in the United States.

Directions: This is the WGLT Challenge. Solve the cryptogram. As the puzzle solver, you need to find which number belongs to which character. And this can be pretty challenging! You will need to match the number with the letter. There are some letters given to you below. This will help you solve the other words and unlock more characters. **Good Luck.**

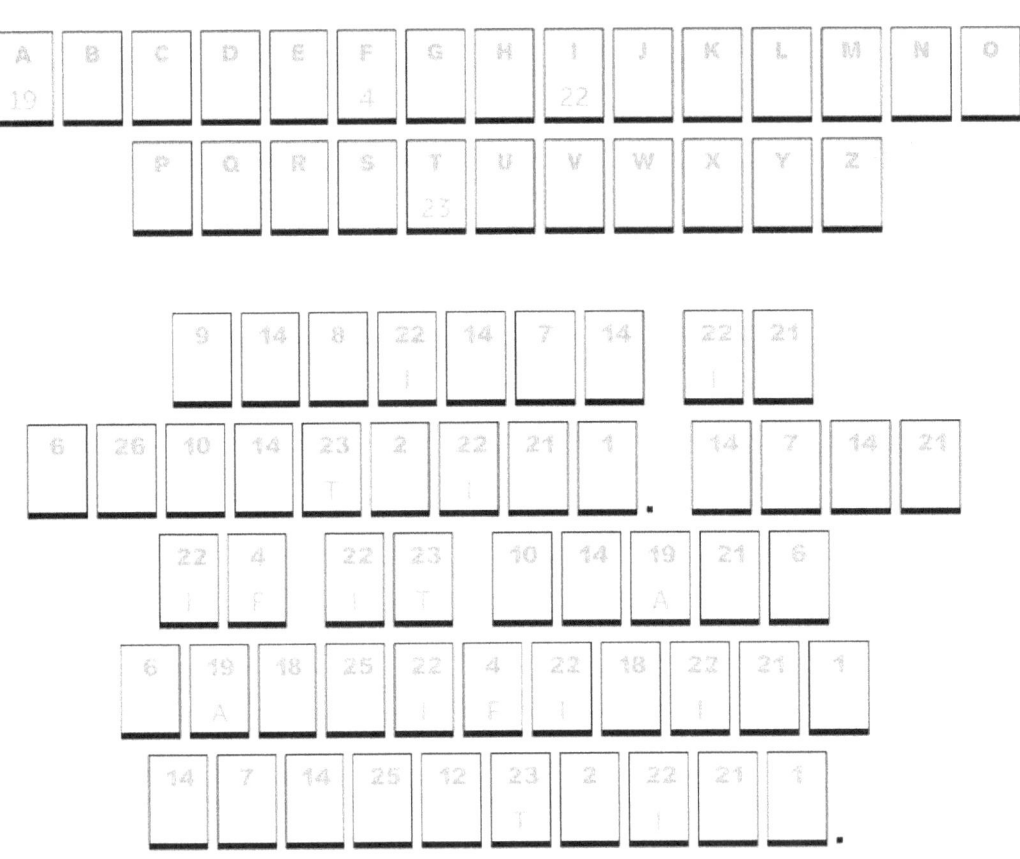

Nelson Mandela

Nelson Mandela

July 18, 1918 – December 5, 2013
PRESIDENT OF SOUTH AFRICA

LEFT BLANK ON PURPOSE

Nelson Mandela

Nelson Mandela

Nelson Mandela

Nelson Mandela

Nelson Mandela

Directions: read the bio below and answer the following questions.

Hi my name is Rolihlahla Mandela. I was born July 18, 1918, in Mvezo in Umtata. No one in my family had ever attended school. On the first day of school my teacher, Miss Mdingane, gave each of us an English name. She told me that my new name was Nelson. I graduated from Methodist High School. I went to college at the University of South Africa where I got my Bachelor's for law in 1943 . I served 27 years in prison for treason and conspiracy against the government. Amid growing domestic and international pressure and fears of racial civil war, President F. W. de Klerk released me in 1990. Me and de Klerk led efforts to negotiate an end to apartheid, which resulted in the 1994 multiracial general election in which I became the first black president of South Africa from 1994 to 1999. I was the country's first black head of state and the first elected in a fully representative democratic election. I was given the nickname "the father of the nation" and "the founding father of democracy".

1. What was my Bachelor's degree in?
    A. Politics
    B. Medical
    C. Law
2. What year did I become president of South Africa?
    A. 1967
    B. 1990
    C. 1994
3. What did I negotiate to end?
    A. Apartheid
    B. Sex Trafficking
    C. Smuggling

Directions: Answer the questions, to solve the crossword puzzle. You can use the internet if you get stuck on any question.

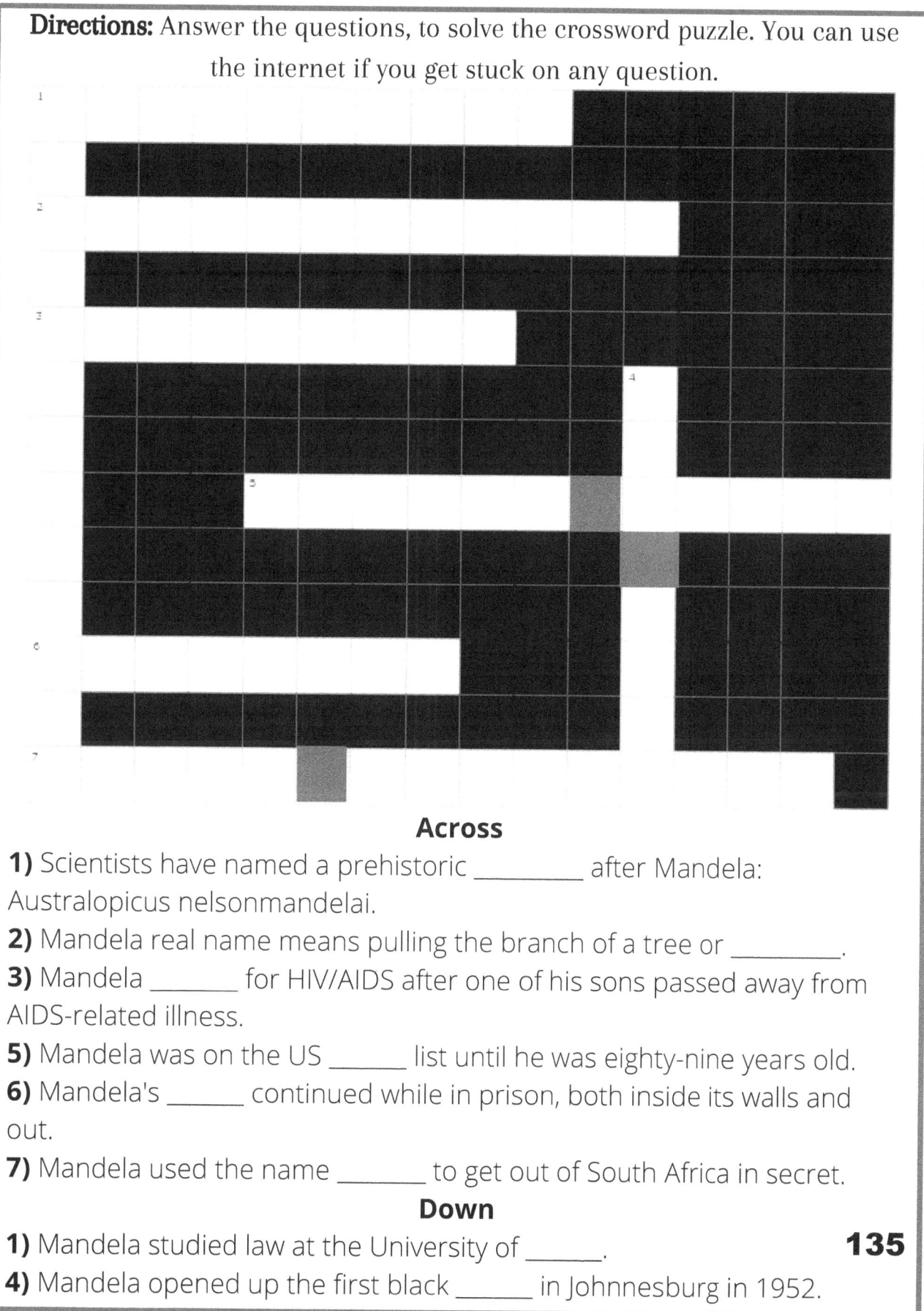

Across

1) Scientists have named a prehistoric _____ after Mandela: Australopicus nelsonmandelai.
2) Mandela real name means pulling the branch of a tree or _____.
3) Mandela _____ for HIV/AIDS after one of his sons passed away from AIDS-related illness.
5) Mandela was on the US _____ list until he was eighty-nine years old.
6) Mandela's _____ continued while in prison, both inside its walls and out.
7) Mandela used the name _____ to get out of South Africa in secret.

Down

1) Mandela studied law at the University of _____.
4) Mandela opened up the first black _____ in Johnnesburg in 1952.

Directions: Read and answer the questions. Nelson facts. Use the internet to help you.

1) What year was Nelson awarded the Nobel Peace Prize.

1990

1993

1995

2) What day is celebrated as Nelson Mandela Day?

August 12th

July 18th

September 28th

3) What political group did Nelson Mandela become a leader of early on in his fight against apartheid?

Democratic National Party

Union of South Africa

African National Congress

4) What is apartheid?

A government system where people were separated by the color of their skin

A set of laws insuring the equal rights of all people

A political party in South Africa

5) How long did Nelson Mandela spend in prison?

26 months

32 years

27 years

6) What type of degree did Nelson Mandela earn from the University of Witwatersrand?

Law

Engineering

History

7) True or False: Nelson Mandela never realized his dream and Apartheid is still practiced in South Africa.

TRUE

FALSE

Directions: Unscramble the words below about Mandela. See if you can get the bonus word.

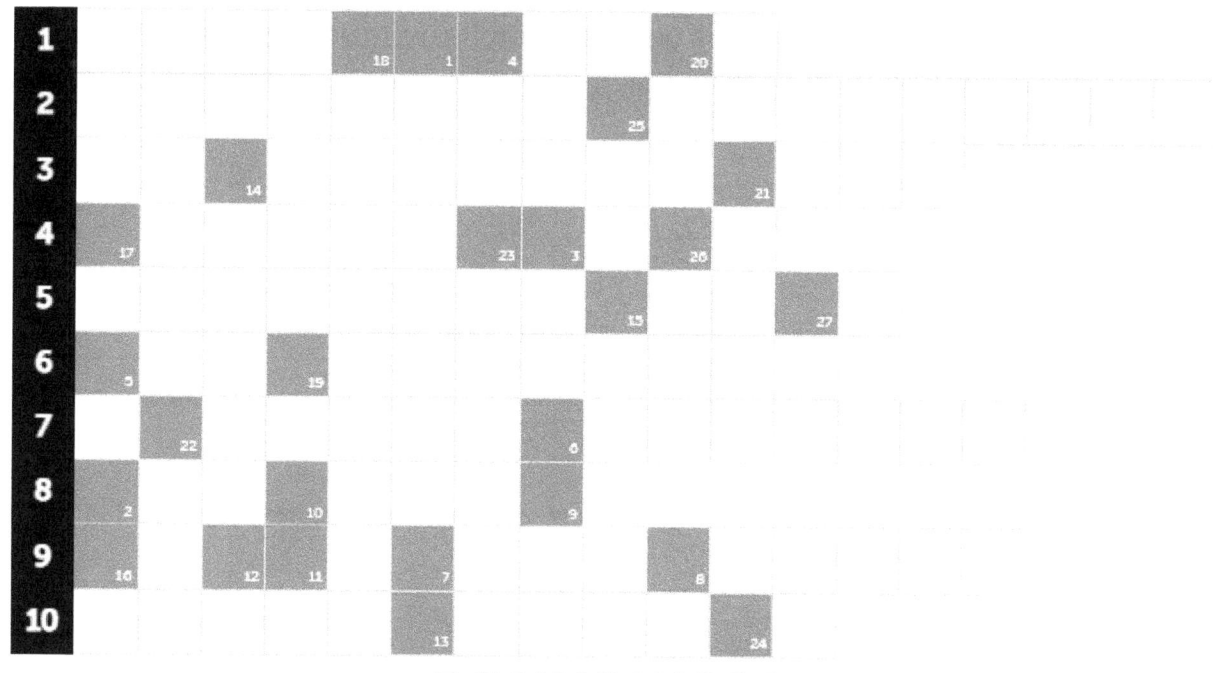

BONUS WORD

Unscramble Words

1) tthfedoaaes
2) cletmnoeotceircida
3) ptreint-daaiah
4) sciohuaftra
5) anncotla-liio
6) talorruebemk
7) ltrdnamapcialee
8) ntivcisu
9) erkkKlrFeerdeid
10) gjnhbnaeuosr

Directions: This is the WGLT Challenge. Solve the cryptogram. As the puzzle solver, you need to find which number belongs to which character. And this can be pretty challenging! You will need to match the number with the letter. There are some letters given to you below. This will help you solve the other words and unlock more characters. **Good Luck.**

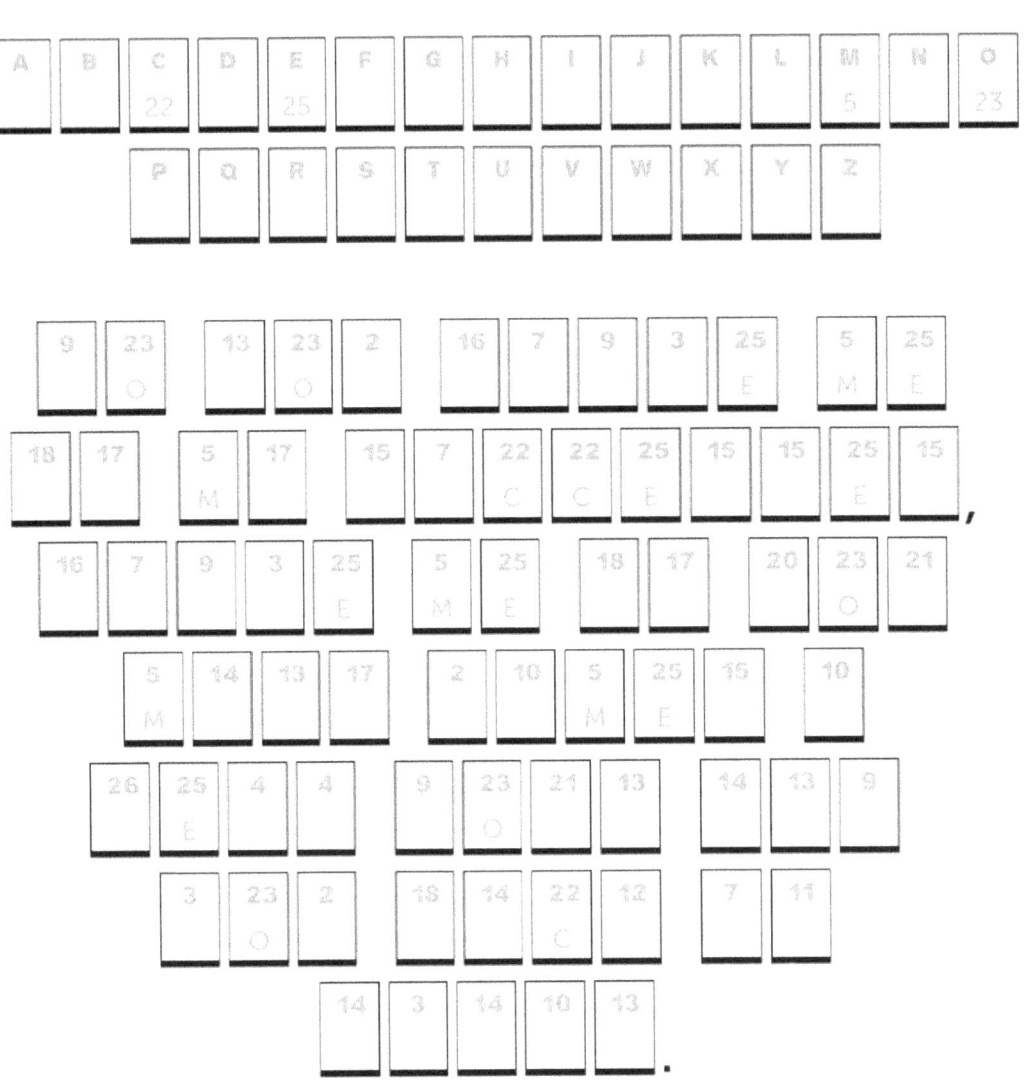

138

Rosa Parks

Rosa Parks

February 4, 1913 – October 24, 2005
CIVIL RIGHTS ACTIVIST

LEFT BLANK ON PURPOSE

Rosa Parks

Rosa Parks

Rosa Parks

Rosa Parks

Rosa Parks

Rosa Parks

Directions: read the bio below and answer the following questions.

Hi, my name is Rosa Parks. I was born on February 4, 1913, in Tuskegee, AL. In 1933, at a time when fewer than 7% of African Americans had a high school diploma, I was able to get mine. In December 1943, I became active in the civil rights movement, joined the Montgomery chapter of the NAACP and was elected secretary. In 1945, despite the Jim Crow laws and discrimination by registrars, I succeeded in registering to vote on my third try. I'm most known for the Montgomery Bus Boycott. I was arrested in 1955 for refusing to give up my seat on the bus to a white man. In 1900, Montgomery passed a city ordinance to segregate bus passengers by race. Conductors were empowered to assign seats to achieve that goal. The Women's Political Council (WPC) decided to hold a sit-in since no one should ride the buses until they were treated with the level of courtesy that they expected. The sit-in lasted 381 days before The U.S. Supreme Court ruled in Browder v. Gayle that it was unconstitutional to segregate public transportation.

1. What was I able to do in 1945?
    A. Ride the bus in any seat
    B. Vote
    C. Join the Military
2. What year did I join the civil rights movement?
    A. 1943
    B. 1950
    C. 1944
3. When was the law passed to segregate the buses?
    A. 1943
    B. 1920
    C. 1900

Directions: Find the words associated with Rosa's life and career.

```
C V Q Q E V C F Q U K T L Z T P T F
S I Q E G H Z O U R R J E A F G Q Q
U U V C K U S C A P I T O L B F T S
S B P I G T R H S R G U W X N S C R
X M A V L V M B N K U A C O T E O K
V O H I J D R I W X D V I X Y G Y F
J N Y L A L I U I J X T C L Q R Y V
H T D R D F N S Q Z C M N Y G E S A
H G R I H G T K O E K O Q E N G U K
R O M G M Q M T S B - T F S M A Y S
T M E H G A C D O S E B X U K T S S
G E H T C I E Y E C H D E X G I R V
F R A S T R S T N P Y D I N Z O C W
W Y X Z O Z I A D D V O A E T N R N
W P C L F H A Q Z M A E B G N L C A
L U O T W C L A T H A U X S Y C S Y
G C K P P A C T I V I S T Y U Q E E
N B T Q G I I E G G V M P G N B C Q
```

Find These Words

CIVILDISOBEDIENCE	COLOREDSECTION	MONTGOMERY
BUSBOYCOTT	CIVILRIGHTS	ACTIVIST
SEGREGATION	NAACP	WHITES-ONLY
USCAPITOL		

Directions: Read and answer the questions. Bus Boycott details. Use the internet to help you.

1) How much was Rosa Parks fined for what she did?

$15

$20

$10

2) In what state did the Montgomery Bus Boycott take place?

Mississippi

Georgia

Alabama

3) What civil rights group did Rosa and her husband Raymond join?

UNIA

NAACP

SCLC

4) According to the article, what did black churches around the country donate to the boycotters?

Shoes

Blanket

Food

5) What did the people of Montgomery do to help support Rosa and to fight back?

They filed a complaint with the city

They boycotted by refusing to ride the city buses

They destroyed most of the city buses

6) How long did the boycott last?

Over a year

Three months

A year and a half

Directions: Read and answer the questions below. There are clues in the puzzle to help you. Try and solve the cryptic message.

Clue for cryptic message: Rosa fought for them to be equal.

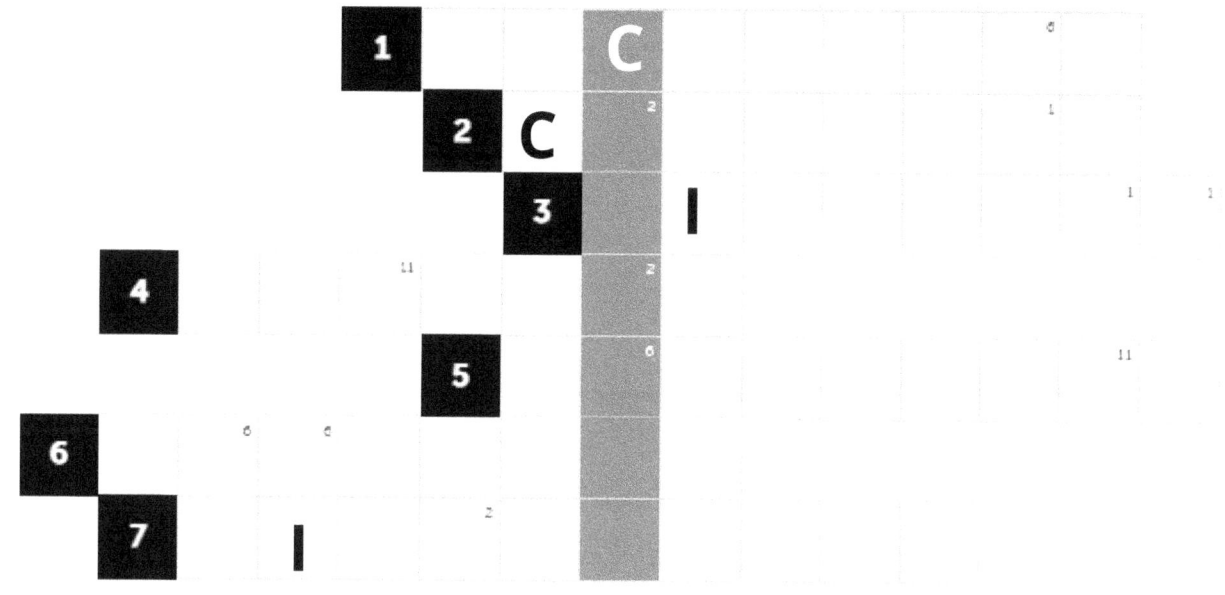

Questions

1) Rosa was the _____ of the local NAACP chapter.
2) The United States _____ has honored Rosa as "the mother of the freedom movement"
3) Rosa was the first African American woman to have her _____ depicted in National Statuary Hall
4) Rosa was awarded the Presidential Medal of _____ , the highest honor given by the US executive branch.
5) Rosa _____ high school in 1933. At this time, less than 7% of African-Americans had a high school diploma.
6) Rosa was not the first African American woman to be _____ for refusing to yield her seat on a Montgomery bus.
7) Rosa found guilty of _____ conduct and violating a local ordinance.

Directions: This is the WGLT Challenge. Solve the cryptogram. As the puzzle solver, you need to find which number belongs to which character. And this can be pretty challenging! You will need to match the number with the letter. There are some letters given to you below. This will help you solve the other words and unlock more characters. **Good Luck.**

Thurgood Marshall

Thurgood Marshall

July 2, 1908 – January 24, 1993
SUPREME COURT JUSTICE/CIVIL RIGHTS ACTIVIST

147

Thurgood Marshall

Thurgood Marshall

Thurgood Marshall

Thurgood Marshall

Thurgood Marshall

Thurgood Marshall

Directions: read the bio below and answer the following questions.

Hi, my name is Thurgood Marshall. I was born on July 2, 1908, in Baltimore, MD. I graduated from Frederick Douglass High School. I graduated from Lincoln University with a Bachelor of Arts in American Literature and Philosophy in 1930. While at Lincoln, I became a member of the Alpha Phi Alpha fraternity. I also graduated magna cum laude from Howard Law in 1933 and ranked first in my class with a Bachelor of Laws (LL.B). After graduating from law school, I started a private law practice in Baltimore. I joined the National Association for the Advancement of Colored People (NAACP) in 1934. President John F. Kennedy appointed me to the United States Court of Appeals for the Second Circuit in 1961. In 1965, President Lyndon B. Johnson appointed me to be the United States Solicitor General. I was the first African American to hold this office. In 1967, I became the first African American to serve as a Supreme Court justice.

1. What fraternity am I a member of?
    A. Omega Psi Phi
    B. Kappa Alpha Psi
    C. Alpha Phi Alpha
2. What year did I get confirmed to the Supreme Court?
    A. 1967
    B. 1961
    C. 1965
3. What college is my BA in literature and philosophy?
    A. Howard University
    B. Lincoln University
    C. Fisk University

Directions: Answer the questions, to solve the crossword puzzle. You can use the internet if you get stuck on any question.

Across

1) _____ replace Thurgood on the Supreme Court when he retired.
5) Thurgood's dad took him to observe _____ at local courts when he was young.
7) Thurgood sued University of _____ to allow black students to attend.
8) Thurgood's nomination to Supreme Court took a year for the Senate to confirm because the _____ of several southern Senators.

Down

2) Thurgood fought for _____ for African-American teachers and won in Maryland.
3) Thurgood won a landmark decision in the Smith v. _____ case which overturned the Texas state law that authorized parties to set their internal rules.
4) Thurgood was an _____ for the FBI, giving information on communist trying to infiltrate the NAACP.
6) Thurgood shorten his birth name Thoroughgood in the ____ grade.

Directions: Read and answer the questions. More on Thurgood's life. Use the internet to help you.

1) Who played in the one-man Broadway play Thurgood in 2008.

James Earl Jones

Laurence Fishburne

Denzel Washington

2) Thurgood was the chief council of what civil rights group?

SCLC

NAACP

UNIA

3) Which president nominated Thurgood for the Supreme Court?

Lyndon Johnson

Richard Nixon

Dwight Eisenhower

4) Which case did Thurgood argue and win in the Supreme Court making it a landmark decision?

Browder v. Gayle

Brown v. Board of Education

Taylor v. Alabama

5) Which president appointed Thurgood as a judge on the United States Court of Appeals.

Gerald Ford

John F. Kennedy

Harry S. Truman

6) Who did Thurgood replace on the Supreme Court.

William J. Brennan Jr.

Potter Stewart

Tom C. Clark

Directions: Unscramble the words below about Thurgood. See if you can get the bonus word.

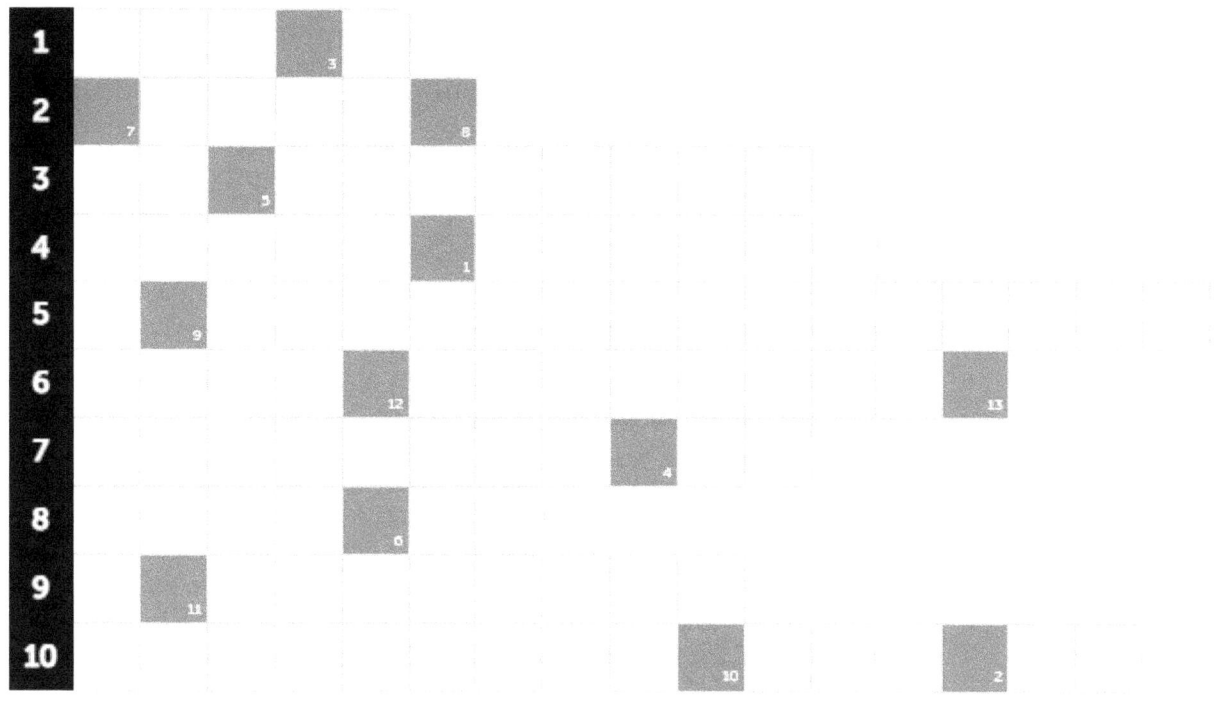

BONUS WORD

Unscramble Words

1) napac
2) wlerya
3) cisvligihrt
4) restomupceru
5) tniyclvuelosinrin
6) furtolpposeaca
7) ertaoegsnig
8) jistcue
9) plpihhsoyo
10) rcltensoirgelaio

153

Directions: This is the WGLT Challenge. Solve the cryptogram. As the puzzle solver, you need to find which number belongs to which character. And this can be pretty challenging! You will need to match the number with the letter. There are some letters given to you below. This will help you solve the other words and unlock more characters. **Good Luck.**

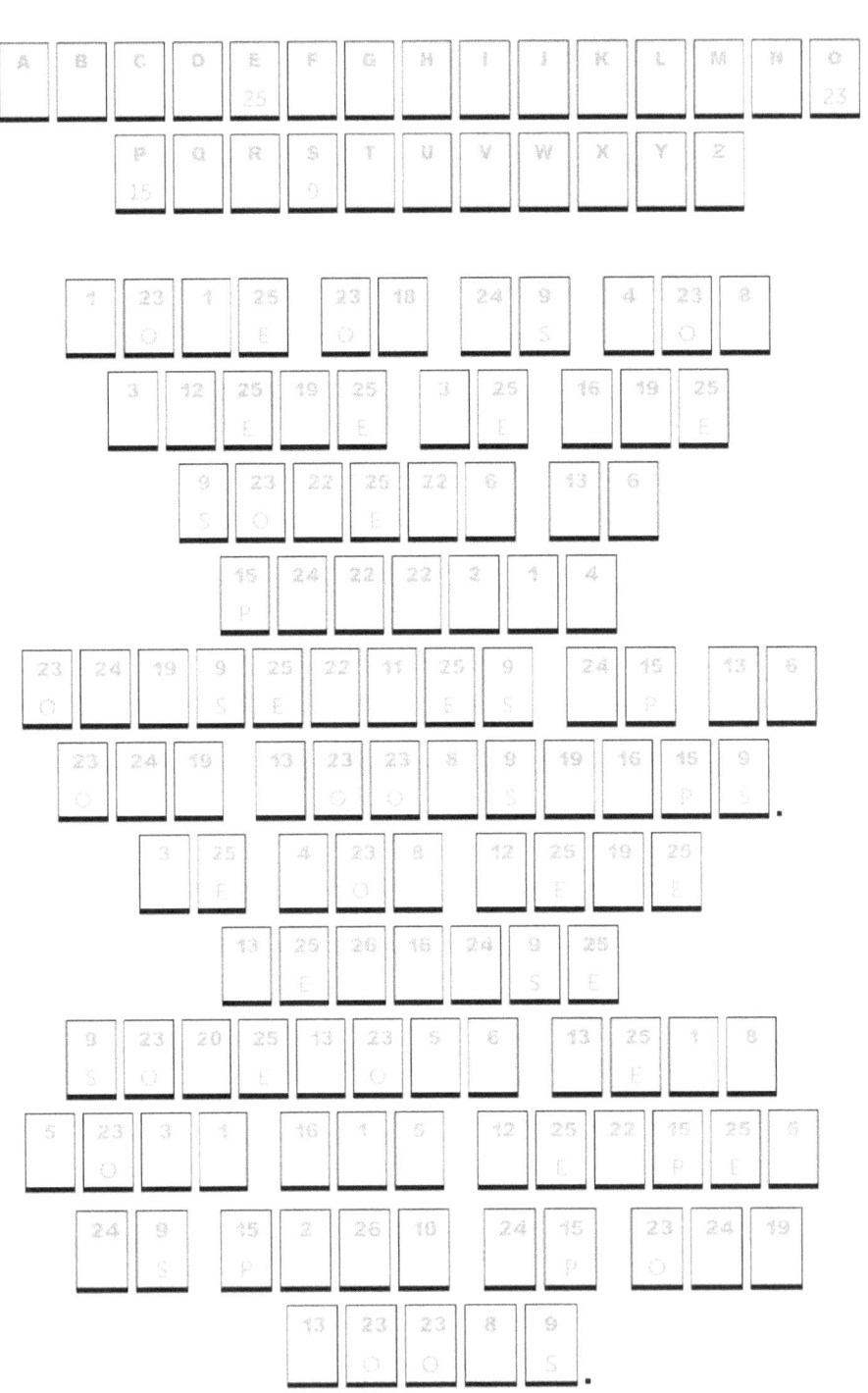

154

Michelle Obama

Michelle Obama

January 17, 1964 - PRESENT
FIRST LADY OF THE UNITED STATES

LEFT BLANK ON PURPOSE

Michelle Obama

Michelle Obama

Michelle Obama

Michelle Obama

Michelle Obama

Michelle Obama

Directions: read the bio below and answer the following questions.

Hi, my name is Michelle Obama. I was born on January 17, 1964, in Chicago, IL. I graduated as a salutatorian from Whitney Young High School. I graduated cum laude with a Bachelor of Arts in 1985 from Princeton University. I earned my Juris Doctor (J.D.) degree from Harvard Law School in 1988. In 1991, I worked as an assistant to the mayor and as the assistant commissioner of planning and development. In 1993, I became the executive director of the Chicago office of Public Allies. In 1996, I served as the associate dean of student services at the University of Chicago, where I developed the university's Community Service Center. In 2002, I began working for the University of Chicago Hospitals, first as the executive director of community affairs and the, beginning in May 2005, as the vice president of community and external affairs. I served as the First Lady of the United States from 2009 to 2017. I was the first African American woman to serve in this position. I'm also an honorary member of Alpha Kappa Alpha (AKA).

1. What college did I get my Juris Doctor from?
   A. Princeton University
   B. Harvard University
   C. Colombia University
2. What University did I work for?
   A. Illinois
   B. New York
   C. Chicago
3. I was the first African-American female to what?
   A. Become President of the United States
   B. Become Vice President of the United States
   C. Become First Lady of the United States

Directions: Find the words associated with Michelle's life and career.

```
Q O F I J X Y R M J P W C O W O W H
E U S W J W P G W T N I N A J F A M
C N P Q Q I X R H K T K I Z H V A O
F O W P L L O V G Y Y Q Y F A H G S
B E C O M I N G H N R J G R V D N T
Q K Y V P Z T A D X K I D K P O K A
F T Z Q V Q L D O O D U W D L M A D
H G R T D L V I N Y N C W P I L Y M
H R T L V M F O A I E C Y E Z D R I
V F Z H G M I L V A H N M K Y S I R
S D Z U E T A E O I W S R G M A V E
T C C B I T R A C T Q P R O B P A D
P O M R P S I A R L U K C G T M B W
S I T F I G G G Y Z O S U E I T D O
C U T T O O F H E G A S H G O V A M
N O Y B J G Y Y U R G C X A T D I A
S P M F D A C E A B R U N K D D W N
X P W Z R O T C E S C I L B U P T U
```

Find These Words

THETIGER	ATTORNEY	FLOTUS
CHICAGO	CITYHALL	MOSTADMIREDWOMAN
HAVARDUNIVERSITY	PUBLICSECTOR	BECOMING
NUTRITION		

Directions: Read and answer the questions. Let's move information. Use the internet to help you.

1) Who did the Healthy, Hunger-Free Kids Act changed nutrition standards for?

Farmers Market Nutrition Program

National School Lunch Program

Child and Adult Care Food Program

2) Which requirement is not a part of the Let's Move program?

fruits

whole grains

cookies

3) Let's Move! initiative to combat childhood obesity.

True

False

4) Who created the first major vegetable garden at the White House.

Michelle Obama

Hillary Clinton

Eleanor Roosevelt

5) Let's Move Active Schools was started so kids could attend schools that strive to make.

Pro Athletes

Sixty minutes of physical activity a day

More yoga classes during gym class

6) Fruits, vegetables and water with no added ingredients are considered Smart Snacks.

True

False

Directions: Read and answer the questions below. There are clues in the puzzle to help you. Try and solve the cryptic message.

Clue for cryptic message: Michelle held this title.

Questions

1) One of Michelle's guilty pleasure foods is _____.

2) Michelle was vice president for _____ and External Affairs at the University Medical Center.

3) Michelle left a career in _____ law to work in public service.

4) Michelle skipped the _____ grade.

5) Michelle was assistant commissioner of planning and _____ in Chicago's City Hall

6) Michelle graduated with a bachelor's in _____ and a minor in African-American studies.

7) Michelle worked the Reach Higher _____ to help students understand job opportunities and the education and skills they need for those jobs.

8) Michelle worked as an _____ for poverty awareness, education and nutrition.

9) Michelle launched the Let's Move campaign to eliminate childhood ___.

Directions: This is the WGLT Challenge. Solve the cryptogram. As the puzzle solver, you need to find which number belongs to which character. And this can be pretty challenging! You will need to match the number with the letter. There are some letters given to you below. This will help you solve the other words and unlock more characters. **Good Luck.**

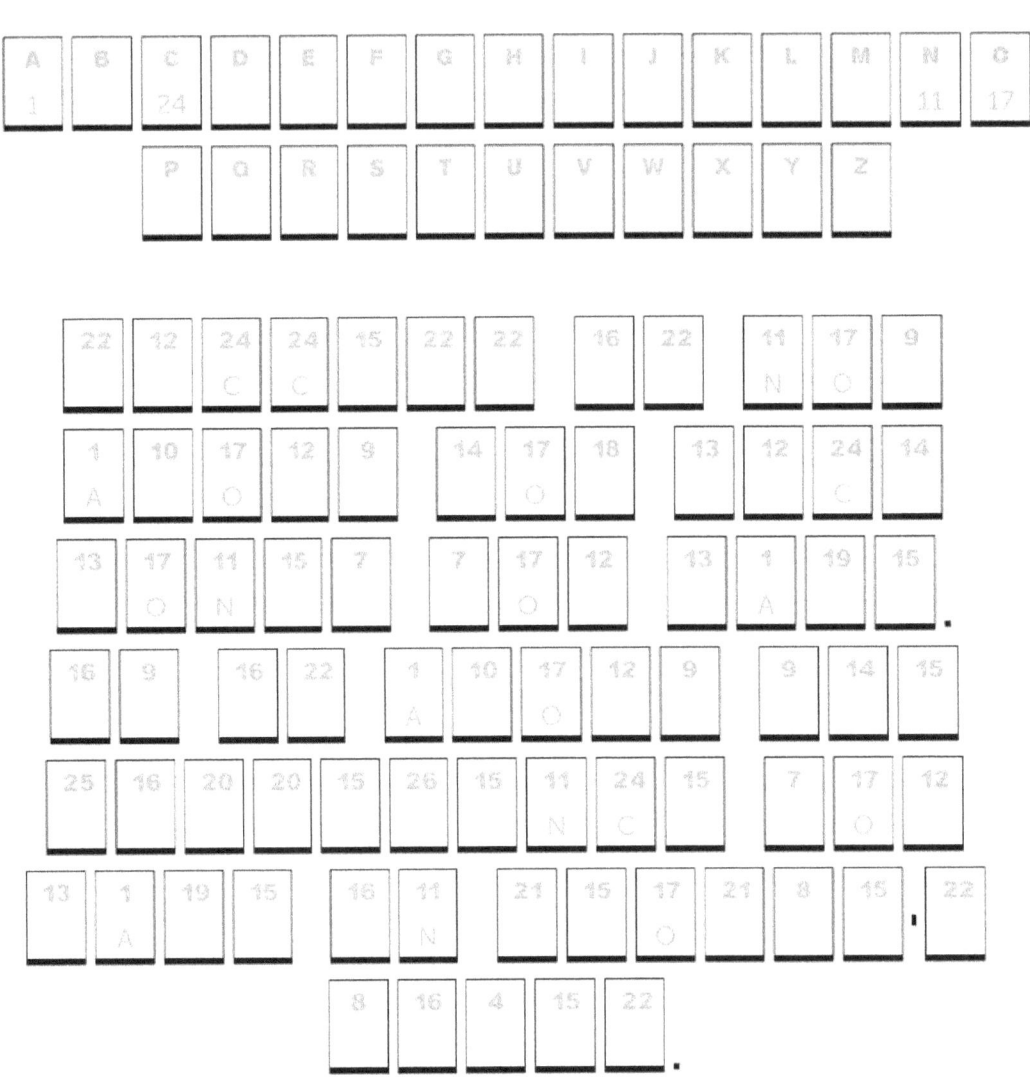

Martin Luther King Jr.

Martin Luther King Jr.

163

January 15, 1929 – April 4, 1968
CIVIL RIGHTS ACTIVIST

LEFT BLANK ON PURPOSE

Martin Luther King Jr

Martin Luther King Jr

Martin Luther King Jr

Martin Luther King Jr

Martin Luther King Jr

Martin Luther King Jr

Directions: read the bio below and answer the following questions.

Hi, my name is Michael King Jr. I was born on January 15, 1929, in Atlanta, GA. My father visited sites in Germany that were associated with the Reformation leader, Martin Luther. What Luther did touched my father so much that he changed our names to Martin Luther King and Martin Luther King, Jr. I attended Booker T. Washington High School but was allowed to attend Morehouse College during my junior year. I graduated from Morehouse with a bachelor's degree in sociology in 1948 when I was 19. I graduated with a Bachelor of Divinity (B. Div.) degree in 1951 from Crozer Theological Seminary. By the time I turned 25, I earned my Ph.D. in systematic theology from Boston University. In 1957, other civil rights activists and I founded the Southern Christian Leadership Conference (SCLC). Some things that I'm known for are the march on Washington, my "I Have a Dream" speech in 1963, the Selma voting rights movement and "Bloody Sunday" in 1965 and my opposition to the Vietnam War.

1. What college didn't I go to?
    A. Boston University
    B. Morehouse College
    C. Clark University
2. What age did I get my Ph.D in systematic theology?
    A. 35
    B. 40
    C. 25
3. What organization did I help found?
    A. SCLC
    B. NAACP
    C. SNCC

Directions: Answer the questions, to solve the crossword puzzle. You can use the internet if you get stuck on any question.

Across
1) Martin was _____ the leader of the Civil Rights Movement during the Montgomery Bus Boycott.
4) Martin was only _____ when he entered his dad's alma mater, Morehouse College.
5) Martin was _____ by James Earl Ray in Memphis, TN.
6) Before getting involved in the civil rights movement, Martin was a _____.
7) Stevie Wonder wrote the song _____ to honor Martin.

Down
1) Martin was in the room when the _____ Act was signed.
2) Martin was the _____ person to win the Nobel Peace Prize in 1964.
3) Martin was introduced to the teachings and philosophies of Mohandas _____ while at Crozer Theological Seminary.

167

Directions: Read and answer the questions. Civil Rights info. Use the internet to help you.

1) What was the name of the laws the southern states used against African-Americans.

Free Speech

Jim Crow

Right to Bear Arms

2) What legislation was passed in 1964 as a result of the March on Washington?

Civil Rights Act

Voter's Rights Act

Fourteenth Amendment

3) What legislation was passed in 1965 as a result of the Selma to Montgomery marches?

Voter's Rights Act

Fifteenth Amendment

Civil Rights Act

4) Martin Luther King, Jr. was arrested more than twenty times.

True

False

5) What Constitutional amendment made slavery illegal?

Fifteenth Amendment

Fourteenth Amendment

Thirteenth Amendment

Directions: Unscramble the words below about Martin. See if you can get the bonus word.

BONUS WORD

Unscramble Words

1) asibttp **2)** vcatstii **3)** inastssosiana
4) felioonrbcpti **5)** oagrgie **6)** byoutstcob
7) uooersemh **8)** hllodiymak **9)** siinmtre
10) oovnnecilen

Directions: This is the WGLT Challenge. Solve the cryptogram. As the puzzle solver, you need to find which number belongs to which character. And this can be pretty challenging! You will need to match the number with the letter. There are some letters given to you below. This will help you solve the other words and unlock more characters. **Good Luck.**

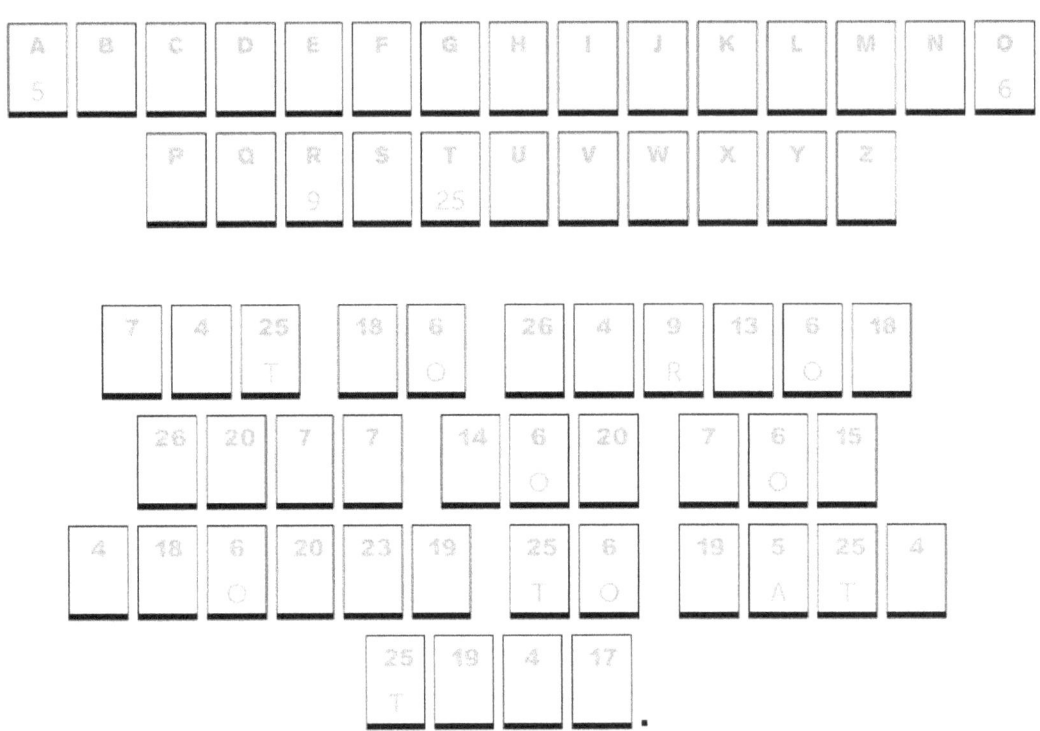

Sojouner Truth

Sojouner Truth

171

1797 – November 26, 1883
ABOLITIONIST

LEFT BLANK ON PURPOSE

Sojouner Truth

Sojouner Truth

Sojouner Truth

Sojouner Truth

Sojouner Truth

Sojouner Truth

Directions: read the bio below and answer the following questions.

Hi, my name is Isabella Baumfree. I was born in 1797 in Swartekill, NY. I was born into slavery. I married an older enslaved man named Thomas. I bore five children: James, my firstborn, who died in childhood, Diana (1815), who was the result of me being raped by John Dumont, Peter (1821), Elizabeth (1825) and Sophia (1826). My youngest three children were born after Thomas and I married. Late in 1826, I escaped to freedom with my infant daughter, Sophia. I had to leave my other children behind because they were not legally freed under the emancipation order until they had served as bound servants into their twenties. I learned that my son Peter had been sold by Dumont and then illegally resold to an owner in Alabama. I took the issue to the New York Supreme Court and won the case. I became one of the first Black women to go to court against a white man and win my case. I changed my name to Sojourner Truth in 1843 after I heard the Spirit of God calling me to preach the truth. I told my friends, "The Spirit calls me and I must go." I traveled and preached about the abolition of slavery.

1. My name before I changed it to Sojourner Truth was?
    A. Sophia Baumfree
    B. Elizabeth Baumfree
    C. Isabella Baumfree
2. What year did I escape being a slave?
    A. 1826
    B. 1821
    C. 1825
3. I was one of the first black women to do what?
    A. Become a free person
    B. Own a house
    C. Win a court case against a white man

Directions: Find the words associated with Sojourner's life and career.

```
S R J V A Z R P I U T Y H S C W X D
B A S A T I W L N C S I L W P C X S
M N W B Q T L L U B C A S N R M U T
H L E R A V G A K L V H Q Y U F P M
Q O G P B P G W T E Z C N S R B O F
Q C R Z O Q F F R E C X V U Z G E K
N N D I L A R Y N V Y Y K P K J D E
V I T Y I P J C W N A M D R B S W U
S L Q T T T Z S V Q H V E E B A G N
W T H A I V R R K I V T Y M A E U I
B N E T O X F Y U Y X O U E M S M O
R E H W N X U T X S R B N C A E N N
F D U Z I V M P H E I Z O O B O W A
I I A B S X W H V I X W R U A S C R
Z S Z N T M C S P P X A K R L L V M
M E R A W L I V I C Y L A T A M Z Y
I R V J V S W K K L J J V S V K J S
T P X J S T H G I R S N E M O W C D
```

Find These Words

WOMENSRIGHTS   ABOLITIONIST   NYSUPREMECOURT
ALABAMA   PRESIDENTLINCOLN   AKRON
CIVILWAR   UNIONARMY   SLAVERY
FAITH

Directions: Read and answer the questions. Sojourner speeches. Use the internet to help you.

1) What did Sojourner do to stop a band of young men from tearing up the camp meeting?

Fought them

Sang a song

Nothing she could do

2) What city did Sojourner speak at for the annual antislavery convention in the 1840's?

Chicago

Philadelphia

Boston

3) How many parts did Sojourner speech have at the American Equal Rights Association in 1867.

Three

One

Five

4) Sometimes Sojourner was greeted how when they announced her as a speaker?

Throwing things

Walking out

Hissing and Groaning

5) What were people called who wanted to bring about an end to slavery?

Communists

Abolitionist

Capitalist

Directions: Read and answer the questions below. There are clues in the puzzle to help you. Try and solve the cryptic message.

Clue for cryptic message: Sojourner recruited for them.

Questions

1) Sojourner spoke _____ when she was growing up.

2) NASA named the Mars _____ rover Sojourner.

3) Sojourner helped recruit black troops for the _____ War.

4) Sojourner gave a speech called "Ain't I a _____" at the Ohio Women's Rights Convention in Akron, Ohio.

5) Sojourner was invited to the White House by President _____.

6) Sojourner is listed among the top 100 All-Time _____ Americans by Smithsonian magazine.

7) Sojourner worked for the National Freedman's _____ Association in Washington, D.C.

8) Sojourner fought to get her son from a slave owner in _____ and won.

9) Sojourner spoke about faith, women's rights and the abolition of _____.

177

Directions: This is the WGLT Challenge. Solve the cryptogram. As the puzzle solver, you need to find which number belongs to which character. And this can be pretty challenging! You will need to match the number with the letter. There are some letters given to you below. This will help you solve the other words and unlock more characters. **Good Luck.**

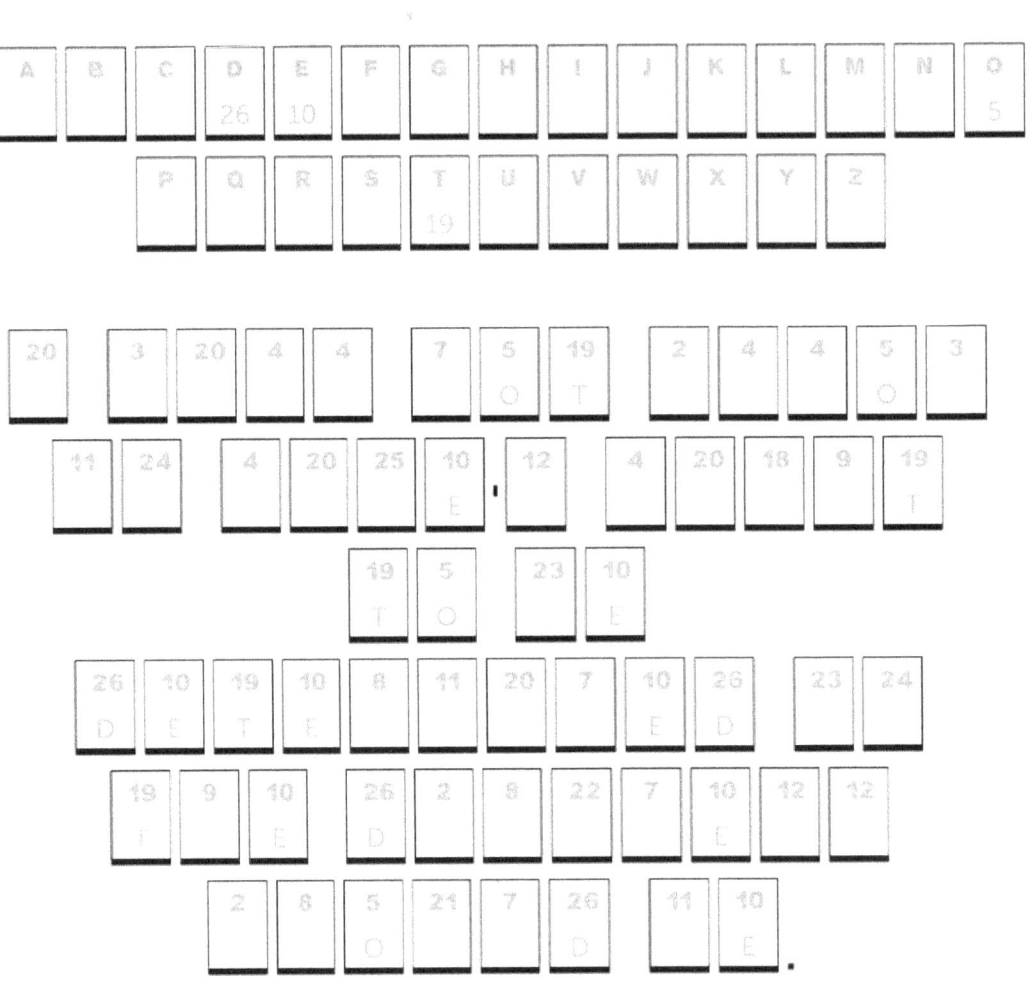

Huey Newton

Huey Newton

February 17, 1942 – August 22, 1989
REVOLUTIONARY

179

Huey Newton

Huey Newton

Huey Newton

Huey Newton

Huey Newton

Huey Newton

Directions: read the bio below and answer the following questions.

Hi, my name is Huey Newton. I was born on February 17, 1942, in Monroe, LA. I graduated from Oakland Technical High School in 1959 with a diploma. I then attended Merritt College and earned an Associate of Arts degree in 1966. I continued my education at San Francisco Law School and the University of California at Santa Cruz, where I earned a bachelor's degree and a master's degree. In 1980, I completed my Ph.D. in social philosophy at Santa Cruz. I also became a member of the Phi Beta Sigma fraternity. While at Merritt, I played a role in getting the first African American history course adopted as part of the college's curriculum. In 1966, while at Merritt College, Bobby Seale and I co-founded the Black Panther Party for Self Defense (BPP). The BPP was an organization that advocated for the right to self-defense for Black people in the US. The BPP started several social programs in Oakland, such as the Oakland Community School, which provided high-level education to 150 children and the Free Breakfast for Children Program.

1. What is the highest education I achieved?
   A. Masters Degree
   B. Ph.D
   C. Bachelors Degree
2. What is the name of my fraternity?
   A. Phi Beta Sigma
   B. Omega Psi Phi
   C. Kappa Alpha Psi
3. What city was the Free Breakfast for Children Program?
   A. Oakland
   B. San Francisco
   C. Fresno

Directions: Answer the questions, to solve the crossword puzzle. You can use the internet if you get stuck on any question.

Across

1) The Black Panther Party was originally named Black Panther Party for _____.

6) Huey earned a Ph.D. in _____ from the University of California at Santa Cruz.

7) The Black Panther's ran _____ and served free breakfasts to schoolchildren.

8) Huey created the Black Panthers to advocate for African-American _____.

Down

2) When Huey got out of jail in 1971, the Panthers embraced a _____ strategy.

3) Huey ran for _____ of Oakland in 1973.

4) Huey was an author, one of his books is 'A _____ Rage'.

5) Huey helped _____ The Black Panther Party.

183

Directions: read the Ten-Point program.

These are the things that the Black Panther Party wanted

1. We want freedom. We want power to determine the destiny of our Black community.
2. We want full employment for our people.
3. We want an end to the robbery by the White man of our Black community.
4. We want decent housing, fit for shelter [of] human beings.
5. We want education for our people that exposes the true nature of this decadent American society. We want education that teaches us our true history and our role in the present day society.
6. We want all Black men to be exempt from military service.
7. We want an immediate end to police brutality and murder of Black people.
8. We want freedom for all Black men held in federal, state, county and city prisons and jails.
9. We want all Black people when brought to trial to be tried in court by a jury of their peer group or people from their Black communities. As defined by the constitution of the United States.
10. We want land, bread, housing, education, clothing, justice and peace.

What are your thoughts

Directions: Unscramble the words below about Huey. See if you can get the bonus word.

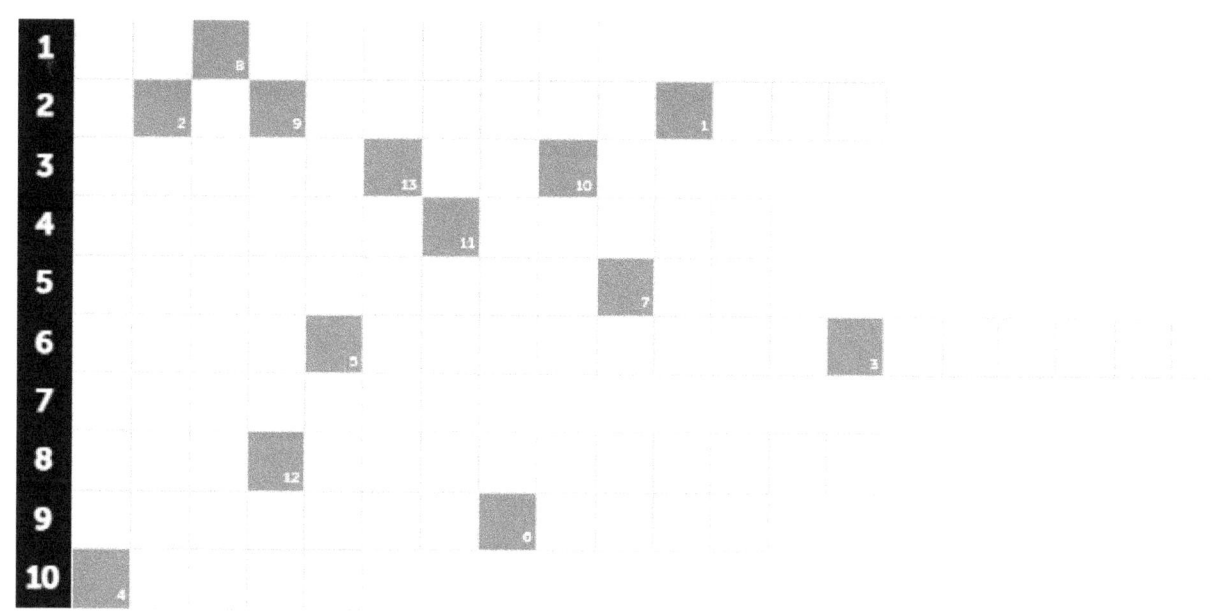

BONUS WORD

1　2　3　4　5　6　7　8　9　10　11　12　13

Unscramble Words

1) tmosfeain　　**2)** teculaorsilpbp　　**3)** yphlopiosh
4) dsen-flsefee　　**5)** nalvyutioerr　　**6)** igkacfluamirarllelyb
7) ladakno　　**8)** ltcteogelirmer　　**9)** reofeyrmdtap
10) hanic

Directions: This is the WGLT Challenge. Solve the cryptogram. As the puzzle solver, you need to find which number belongs to which character. And this can be pretty challenging! You will need to match the number with the letter. There are some letters given to you below. This will help you solve the other words and unlock more characters. **Good Luck.**

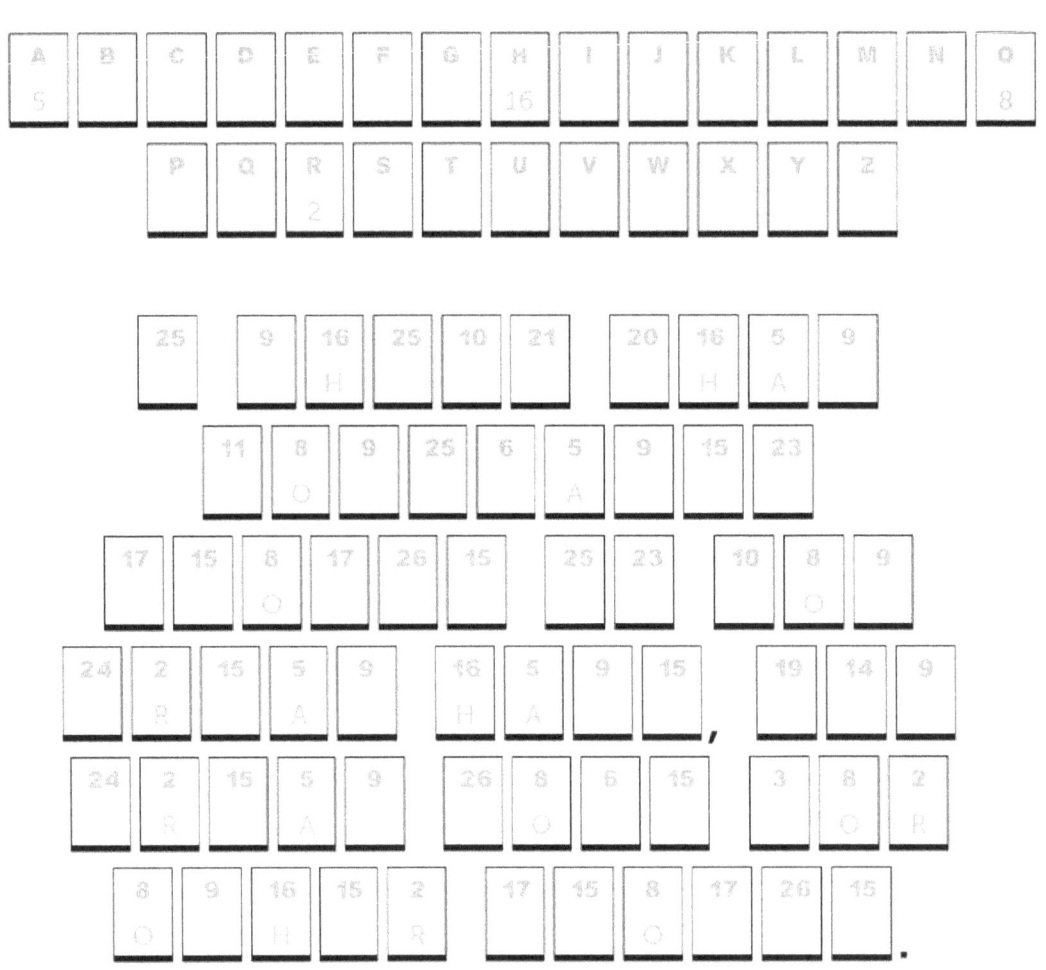

Iyanla Vanzant

Iyanla Vanzant

September 13, 1953 - PRESENT
INSPIRATIONAL SPEAKER

Iyanla Vanzant

Iyanla Vanzant

Iyanla Vanzant

Iyanla Vanzant

Iyanla Vanzant

Iyanla Vanzant

Directions: read the bio below and answer the following questions.

Hi, my name is Rhonda Harris. I was born on September 13, 1953, in Brooklyn, NY. I graduated from the City University of New York School of Law with a Juris Doctorate. I got my master's degree from the University of Santa Monica's Center for the Study and Practice of Spiritual Psychology. I'm also an ordained New Thought minister. From 1988 to 1992, I worked as a public defender in Philadelphia, PA. In 1991, the International Congress of Black Women awarded me an "ONI" as one of the nation's unsung heroines. I was a radio host before I appeared 20 times on The Oprah Winfrey Show from 1998-1999. Some of my achievements include Women's Day magazine listing me as one of the 100 Most Influential Women in the US in 2003. The next year, Ebony magazine named me one of the 100 Most Influential African Americans. In 2012, Watkins Mind Body Spirit Magazine called me one of the 100 most spiritually influential living people. I'm an honorary member of the Alpha Kappa Alpha (AKA) sorority.

1. What University did I get my Juris Doctorate from?
    A. State University of New York
    B. New York University
    C. City University of New York
2. What did I do before I appeared on Oprah's Show?
    A. Day time TV
    B. Radio
    C. Movies
3. What city was I a Public Defender in?
    A. Philadelphia
    B. Brooklyn
    C. Manhattan

Directions: Find the words associated with Iyanla's life and career.

```
M E D G A R E V E R S C O L L E G E
C A W W N F N J G V R O Q E Z M F G
X Q W Y Y B W I Y P S Z P T A K C U
X S A Z E Y W F T P F L X B U Z F N
S N Y Q R D Q N E U A A N F T M D I
B O N R Q A H A U W V K Z D H J T W
A I O M H A K R Y J G M W D O C N A
V S B Y E E M E W O Z I Y H R P A S
H I E H R D R Q L W O D N N W Z W F
F V B C R Q I W N E H U G R W W W C
Z R N M Z T Y T E H C A O C E F I L
G E W Y O Z W X A L U J Z S N C Z H
H N D D Z K P F X T Y J N T A P P I
O N N D P O K P P W I L V N Y O U W
M I S Q M P X A C T S O F F A C T Y
P L Q F U O L X P U B R N L S K R G
B E W H B J M U I F A R J S G K G I
C O P R A H W I N F R E Y S H O W G
```

Find These Words

LIFECOACH   AUTHOR   LAWYER
SPEAKER   MEDITATIONS   INNERVISIONS
OPRAHWINFREYSHOW   ACTSOFFACT   EBONY
MEDGAREVERSCOLLEGE

Directions: Read and answer the questions. Public Speaking Use the internet to help you.

1) What do you love most about speaking?

2) How much do you enjoy being the center of attention?

3) Give some examples on your preparation of a speech?

4) Time to go on stage what do you do?

5) Is the body the major part of a speech?
True
False

6) What is the closing of a speech known as?
Conclusion
A Cut
Ending

Directions: Read and answer the questions below. There are clues in the puzzle to help you. Try and solve the cryptic message.

Clue for cryptic message: Iyanla does this for a living.

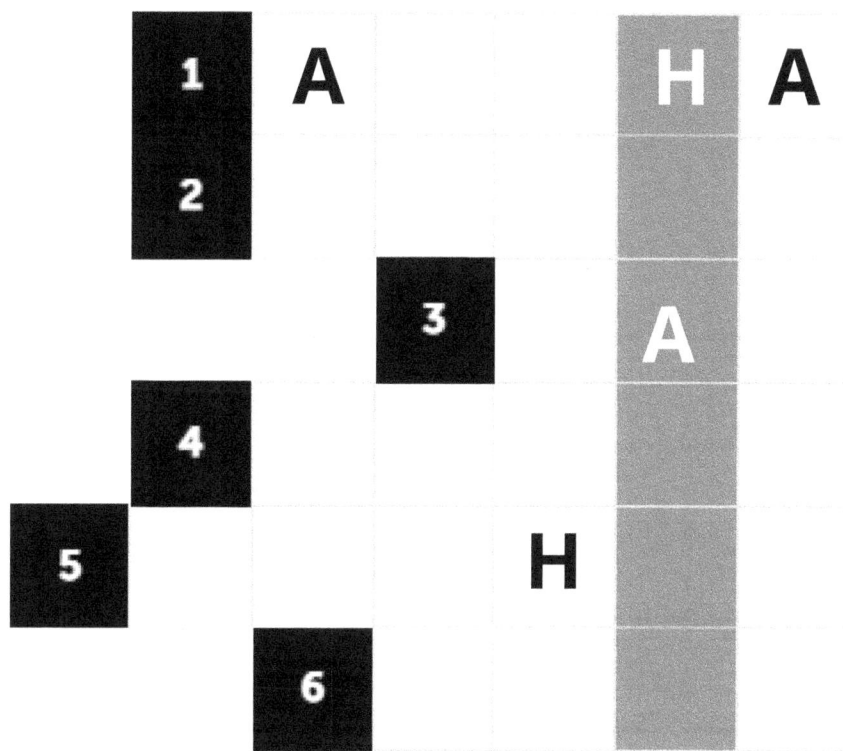

Questions

1) Iyanla is an honorary member of ____ Kappa Alpha sorority.
2) Iyanla has her own TV show called Fix My ____ on the OWN network.
3) Iyanla used to be a ____.
4) Iyanla made a cameo in the movie ____ Trip.
5) Iyanla means 'great _____'.
6) Iyanla is a New ____ Times best-selling author.

Directions: This is the WGLT Challenge. Solve the cryptogram. As the puzzle solver, you need to find which number belongs to which character. And this can be pretty challenging! You will need to match the number with the letter. There are some letters given to you below. This will help you solve the other words and unlock more characters. **Good Luck.**

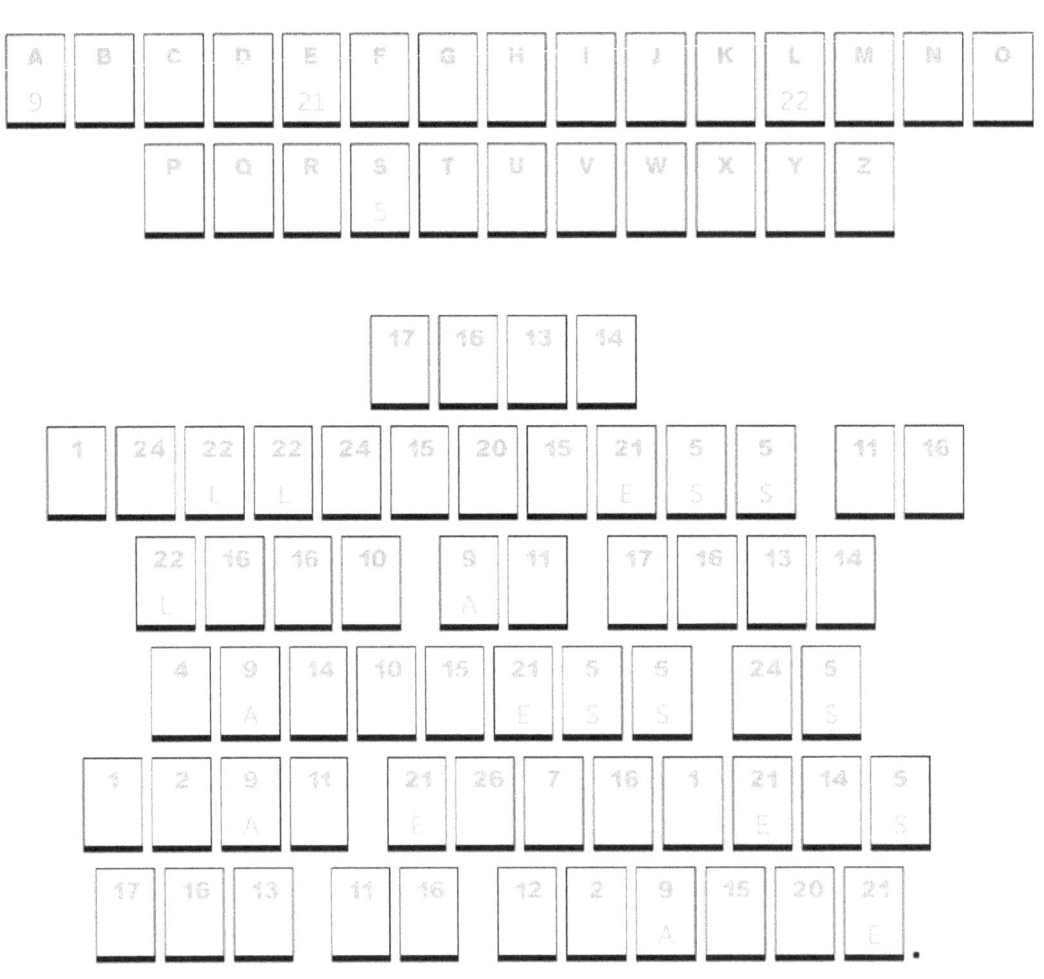

Claudette Colvin

Claudette Colvin

September 5, 1939 - PRESENT
CIVIL RIGHTS ACTIVIST

195

Claudette Colvin

Claudette Colvin

Claudette Colvin

Claudette Colvin

Claudette Colvin

Claudette Colvin

Directions: read the bio below and answer the following questions.

Hi, my name is Claudette Austin. I was born on September 5, 1939, in Montgomery, AL. When I was young, I referred to my great aunt and uncle as my parents, so I took their last name (Colvin). I attended Booker T. Washington High School. On March 2, 1955, I was returning home from school on the bus. I sat in the colored section. The bus became crowded, so we were asked to move. When I refused, the cops were called and I was arrested. I was convicted of disturbing the peace, violating the city's segregation ordinance and assaulting policemen. In response to my conviction, some local community members initiated a boycott of the local bus system. This is better known as the Montgomery Bus Boycott. The NAACP appealed my conviction and filed a lawsuit on my behalf and the behalf of four other women. The case Browder v. Gayle went to the United States Supreme Court on appeal by the state and the court upheld the district court's ruling that bus segregation in Alabama was unconstitutional. After the case, I was branded a troublemaker, so I withdrew from college and moved to New York, where I found a job as a nurse's aide in a nursing home. I worked there for 35 years and retired in 2004.

1. What was the name of my court case?
    A. Colvin v. Montgomery
    B. Austin v. Colvin
    C. Browder v Gayle
2. What did the local's do when I got convicted?
    A. Protest at the Police Station
    B. Boycott the Police Station
    C. Boycott the Bus System
3. What did the bus boycott become known as?
    A. Rosa Parks Movement
    B. Montgomery Bus Boycott
    C. Browder v. Gayle

Directions: Answer the questions, to solve the crossword puzzle. You can use the internet if you get stuck on any question.

Across

1) Claudette case Browder vs Gayle was what ended the Montgomery _____ in December 1956.

3) Claudette moved to New York and got a job as a _____.

5) Claudette attended the Booker T. Washington _____.

6) Claudette incident happened ___ months before the same event happened to Rosa Parks.

7) Claudette reason for not getting up, she said "It's my _____ to sit here as much as that lady. I paid my fare".

8) Claudette was _____ when she was arrested for refusing to give up her seat to a white passenger in a segregated bus.

Down

2) Claudette was a member of the _____ of the National Association for the Advancement of Colored People (NAACP).

4) Claudette is one of the ___ plaintiffs in the Browder v. Gayle case.

Directions: Read and answer the questions. Browder v. Gayle facts. Use the internet to help you.

1) Which federal judge did not rule in Browder v Gayle?

Judge Frank Minis Johnson

Judge Kristi DuBose

Judge Richard Rives

2) How many plaintiffs were apart of the Browder v Gayle case?

One

Five

Three

3) How long did the Bus Boycott last?

30 days

256 days

381 days

4) What year was the Browder v Gayle case resolved?

December 17, 1956

June 5, 1956

November 13, 1956

5) Who was the Mayor at the time of this case.

A. W. Gayle

R. A. Gayle

W. A. Gayle

Directions: Unscramble the words below about Claudette. See if you can get the bonus word.

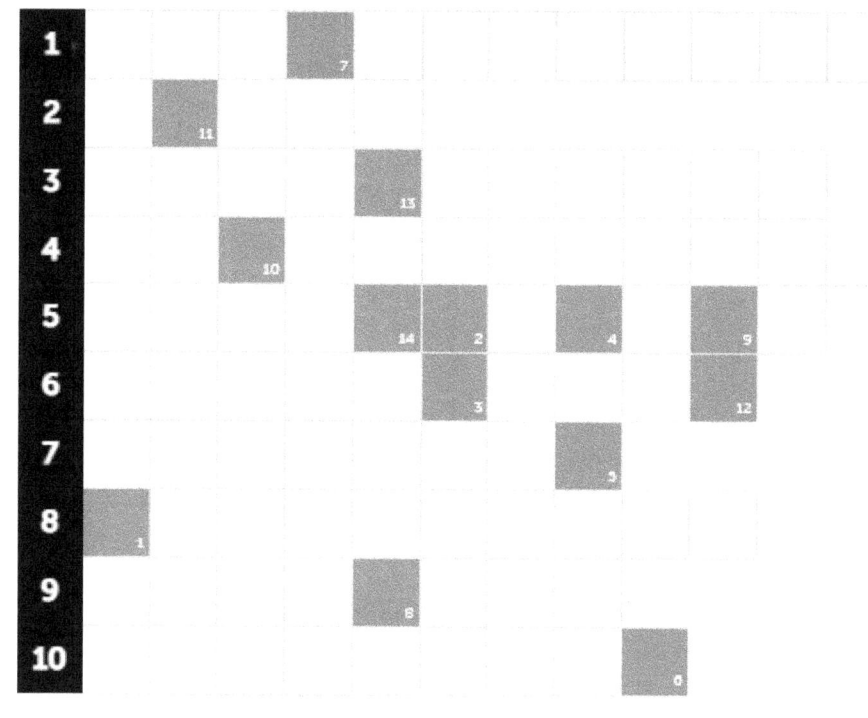

BONUS WORD

Unscramble Words

1) rpumescturoe
2) ncpaa
3) stlviicrihg
4) tosigngaree
5) nbwoiotnastreogkh
6) oegyomtnrm
7) xdeepnug
8) cotosbbuyt
9) vsiatitc
10) eaneursdi

Directions: This is the WGLT Challenge. Solve the cryptogram. As the puzzle solver, you need to find which number belongs to which character. And this can be pretty challenging! You will need to match the number with the letter. There are some letters given to you below. This will help you solve the other words and unlock more characters. **Good Luck.**

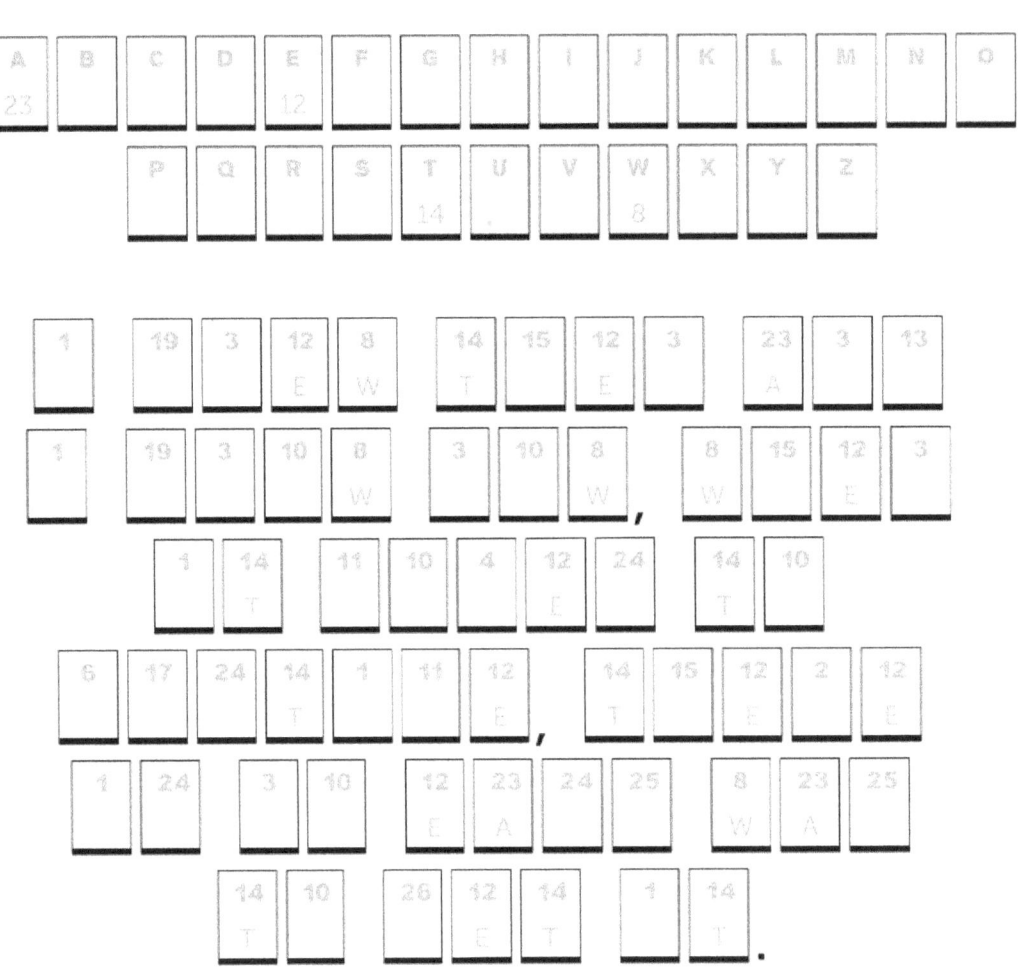

202

1. What was my mother's nickname for me?
   A. Moses
   B. General Tubman
   C. Minty
2. What year did I escape being a slave?
   A. 1849
   B. 1848
   C. 1844
3. What branch did I work for?
   A. Marine Corps
   B. Navy
   C. Union Army

Araminta Ross

Answers

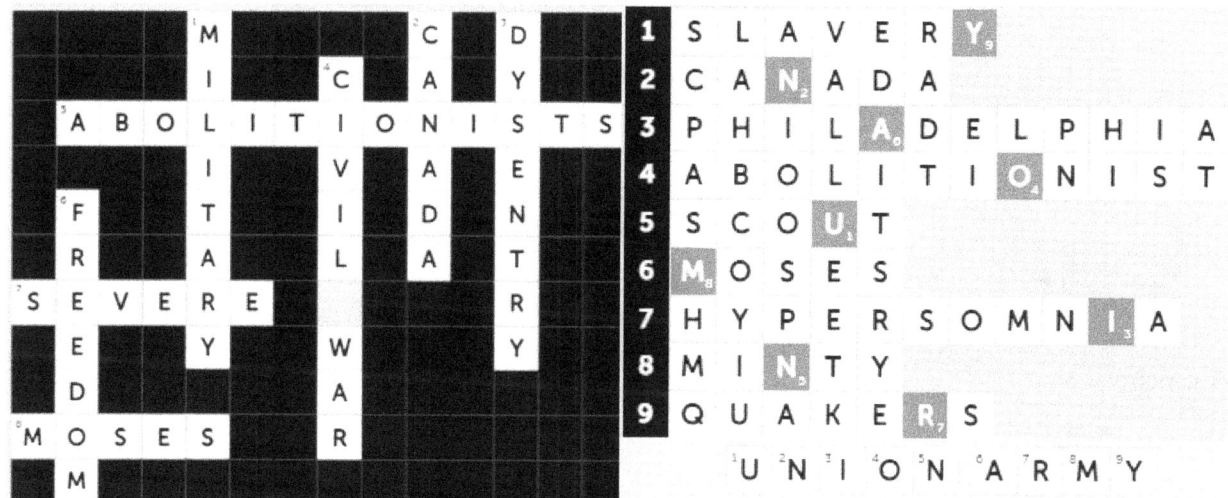

203

John Lewis Answers

1. **What was my degree in?**
   A. Education
   B. Computer Science
   C. Religion and Philosophy
2. **What is the name of my fraternity?**
   A. Alpha Phi Alpha
   B. Omega Phi Psi
   C. Phi Beta Sigma
3. **What branch of the government did I represent?**
   A. U.S. House of Representatives
   B. Senate
   C. Executive

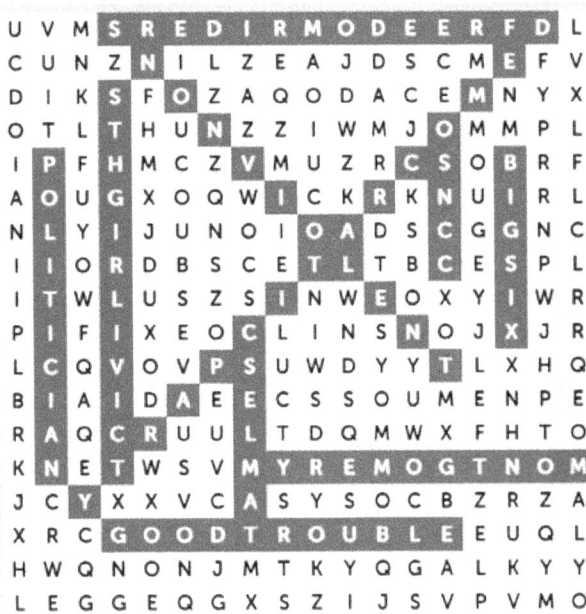

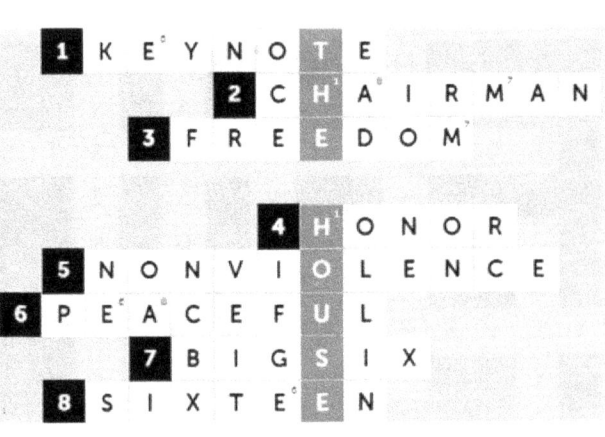

LEGISLATIVE
- Makes laws.
- Approves presidential appointments.
- Two senators from each state.
- Number of congressmen based on population of each state.

EXECUTIVE
- Signs laws.
- Vetoes laws.
- Pardons people.
- Appoints federal judges.
- Elected every four years.

JUDICIAL
- Decides if laws are constitutional.
- Appointed by the president.
- There are 9 justices.
- Can overturn rulings by other judges.

204

1. What was Bachelor degree in?
   A. Childhood Education
   B. Sociology
   C. Computer Science
2. What year did I get elected to Congress?
   A. 1968
   B. 1972
   C. 1983
3. How old was I when I went Barbados?
   A. 10
   B. 3
   C. 5

Shirley Chisholm
Answers

Presidential Powers
1) laws
2) supports
3) armed forces   nuclear weapons
4) president
5) treaties
6) vice president
7) executive
8) vetoed
9) Congress
10) impeached

Crossword:
- NURSERY
- COLUMBIA
- HALL OF FAME
- CONGRESS
- VETERANS' AFFAIRS
- CANDIDACY
- BLACK CAUCUS

1. CONGRESS
2. NEW YORK
3. DEMOCRATIC
4. NURSERY
5. GREAT DEPRESSION
6. BROOKLYN
7. COLUMBIA
8. STATE ASSEMBLY
9. FOREVER STAMP
10. PRESIDENTIAL CAMPAIGN

A	B	C	D	E	F	G	H	I	J	K	L	M	N	O	P	Q	R	S	T	U	V
19	23	13	10	18	7	9	26	14	24	2	17	11	6	5	15	4	25	12	20	8	1

W	X	Y	Z
16	22	3	21

"WE MUST REJECT NOT ONLY THE STEROTYPES THAT OTHERS HAVE OF US BUT ALSO THOSE THAT WE HAVE OF OURSELVES."

205

Nat Turner Answers

1. **Who turned me on to reading the Bible?**
   A. Mother
   B. Grandmother
   C. Father
2. **How old was I when I escaped?**
   A. 18
   B. 15
   C. 21
3. **Why did we rebel?**
   A. To learn ho to read and write
   B. To get married
   C. To escape slavery

How the branches work
1) The House of Representatives and the Senate
2) Judicial Branch, Executive Branch and Legislative in any order
3) speaker
4) senate
5) two
6) vice president
7) house of representatives
8) six
9) two
10) President servers for four years.
11) The answers will vary Example: to make sure there are checks and balancing.

Word search answers: SLAVEHOLDER, PLANTATION, SLAVERECLIPSE, REBELLION, INSURRECTION (and others hidden), RELIGION

Crossword:
1. FILMS
2. RELIGIOUS
3. ERUPTION
4. DIVINELY
5. INSURRECTION
6. TEACH
7. REBELLION
8. WRITE

(Down: MINISTER)

Cipher key:
A=17, B=16, C=4, D=8, E=11, F=15, G=12, H=26, I=24, J=6, K=7, L=18, M=22, N=14, O=9, P=10, Q=19, R=21, S=23, T=1, U=13, V=3, W=20, X=5, Y=25, Z=2

GOOD COMMUNICATIONS
THE BRIDGE BETWEEN
CONFUSION AND CLARITY

206

Fannie Lou Townsend
Answers

1. How old was I when I left school?
   A. 15
   B. 12
   C. 10
2. What year did I register to vote?
   A. 1962
   B. 1963
   C. 1961
3. What party did I represent?
   A. Independent
   B. Republican
   C. Democrat

The Fifteenth Amendment answers

1) An amendment to the U.S. Constitution that banned discriminatory voter registration practices
2) Laws that limited the social and working rights of African Americans.
3) Voting Rights Act
4) Disenfranchisement

Crossword 1 (down/across):
- EDUCATE
- DEMOCRATIC
- VOTING
- FREEDOM
- CIVIL-RIGHTS
- CO-FOUNDER
- DELEGATION
- SECRETARY

Crossword 2:
1. WOMEN RIGHTS
2. VOTERS
3. DEMOCRAT
4. MISSISSIPPI
5. GRASSROOTS
6. TUMOR
7. EQUALITY
8. LITERACY TEST
9. POLL TAX
10. HALL OF FAME
11. FREEDOM SUMMER

Cipher key:
A=17, B=9, C=2, D=22, E=19, F=13, G=3, H=23, I=15, J=24, K=14, L=11, M=5, N=26, O=18, P=1, Q=20, R=16, S=25, T=21, U=4, V=12, W=7, X=8, Y=10, Z=6

Decoded message:
NEVER FORGET WHERE WE CAME FROM AND ALWAYS PRAISE THE BRIDGES THAT CARRIED YOU OVER.

207

Frederick Bailey Answers

1. What year did I escape slavery?
   A. 1840
   B. 1818
   C. 1838
2. What was the name of my newspaper?
   A. Washington Post
   B. New York Times
   C. The North Star
3. What president did I help influence?
   A. Andrew Johnson
   B. Abraham Lincoln
   C. James Buchanan

Thirteenth Amendment answers

1. Abolitionists
2. Abraham Lincoln
3. Civil War
4. Made slavery illegal

Crossword:
1. POEM
2. WRITE
3. ARMY
4. CONVENTION
5. SAILOR
6. PHOTOGRAPHED

Cryptogram: IT IS EASIER TO BUILD STRONG CHILDREN THAN TO REPAIR BROKEN MEN.

208

Ella Josephine Baker
Answers

1. **What does NAACP stand for?**
   A. National Association for the Advancement of Colored People
   B. National Association for All Colored People
   C. National Association for Any Colored Person
2. **What did I graduate college as?**
   A. Salutatorian
   B. Valedictorian
   C. Summa Cum Laude
3. **What does SNCC stand for?**
   A. Students Not Coordinating Color
   B. Students New Color Committee
   C. Student Nonviolent Coordinating Committee

Answers for SNCC
1) C. Fight
2) B. Snick
3) C. Voter registration

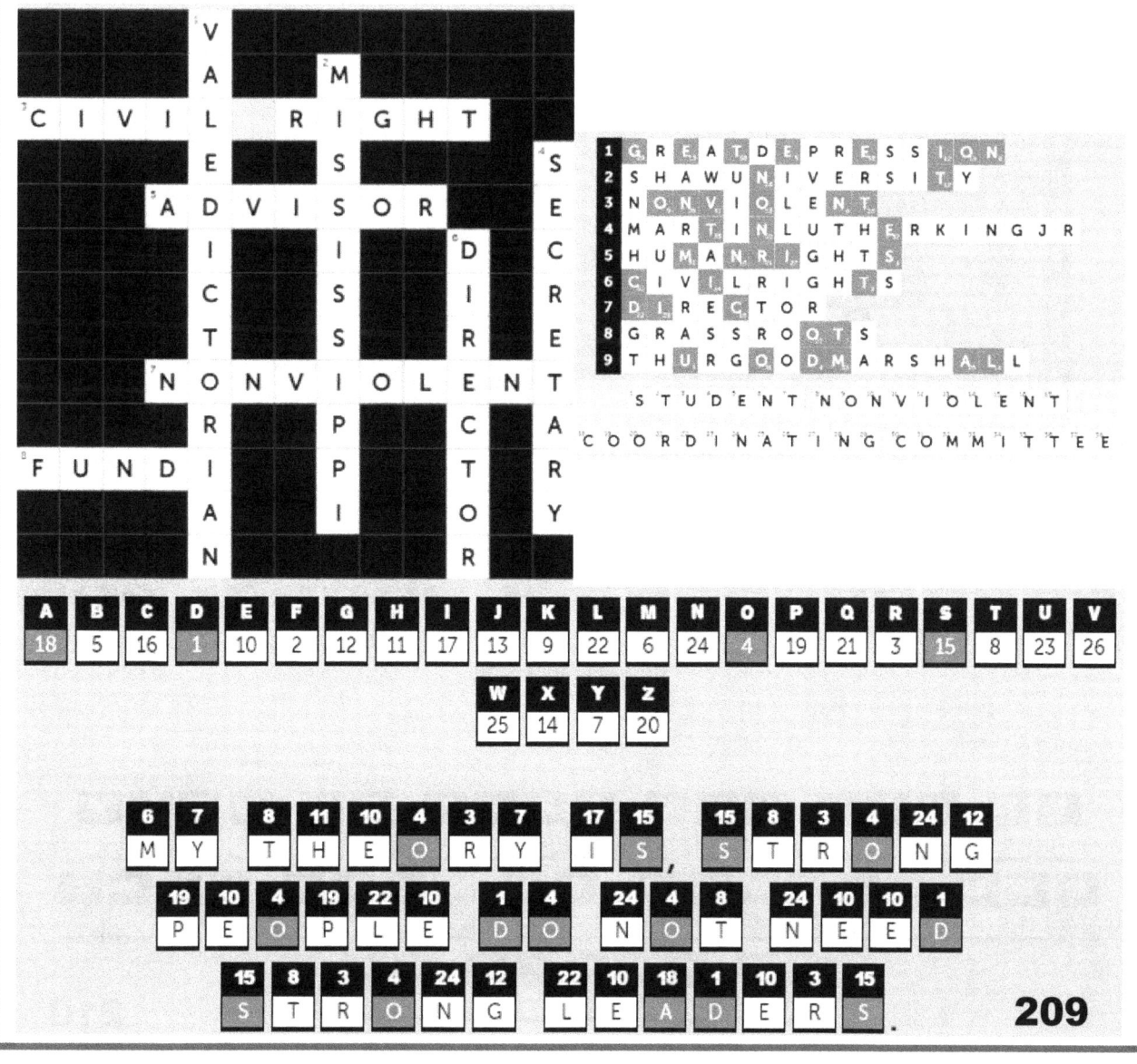

209

Barack Obama
Answers

1. What Law school did I go to?
   A. Columbia
   B. Yale
   C. Harvard
2. In 2008 I was the first African-American to do what?
   A. Become U.S. Senator
   B. Become U.S Congressman
   C. Become U.S President
3. What State did I become a senator of?
   A. Hawaii
   B. Illinois
   C. New York

Questions about the Senate
1) 2
2) 30
3) Vice President of the United States
4) 6 years
5) Legislative
6) They ratify treaties with foreign governments
7) 100
8) Filibuster

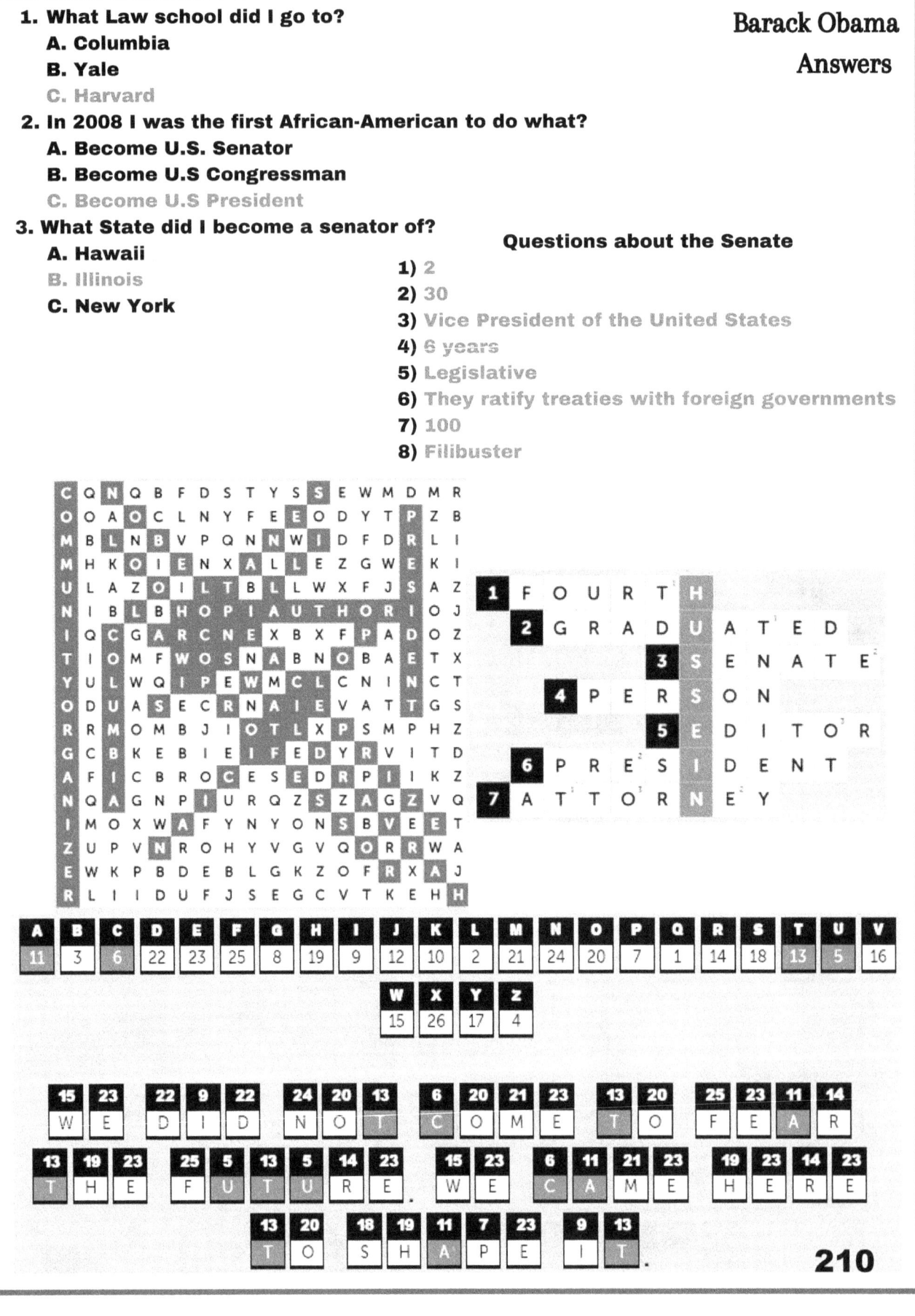

1. FOURTH
2. GRADUATED
3. SENATE
4. PERSON
5. EDITOR
6. PRESIDENT
7. ATTORNEY

A	B	C	D	E	F	G	H	I	J	K	L	M	N	O	P	Q	R	S	T	U	V
11	3	6	22	23	25	8	19	9	12	10	2	21	24	20	7	1	14	18	13	5	16

W	X	Y	Z
15	26	17	4

"WE DID NOT COME TO FEAR THE FUTURE. WE CAME HERE TO SHAPE IT."

210

Angela Davis
Answers

1. What is my highest level of education?
    A. Bachelor Degree
    B. Masters Degree
    C. Ph. D
2. What crime was I accused of?
    A. Theft
    B. Murder
    C. Communist
3. What society did I become a member of after I graduated?
    A. National Honor Society
    B. Phi Beta Kappa
    C. Phi Theta Kappa

13th Amendment answers
1) True
2) Civil War
3) Abolitionists
4) 1995
5) True
6) Made slavery illegal
7) 50%
5) Abraham Lincoln

Crossword answers (across):
- PHILOSOPHER
- WOMENSRIGHTS
- LENINPEACE
- HALLOFFAME
- MURDERFREE
- FRANCE
- EXCLUSION
- MOST WANTED

Word list:
1. DYNAMITEHILL
2. HERBERTMARCUSE
3. EASTGERMANY
4. UNIVERSITYOFCALIFORNIA
5. CRITICALRESISTANCE
6. LENINPEACEPRIZE
7. HALLOFFAME
8. PHILOSOPHER
9. POLITICALACTIVIST
10. SCHOLAR

COMMUNIST PARTY

A	B	C	D	E	F	G	H	I	J	K	L	M	N	O	P	Q	R	S	T	U	V
25	1	10	3	18	4	15	5	26	21	23	22	6	8	24	12	16	11	13	2	9	7

W	X	Y	Z
14	20	17	19

I'M NO LONGER ACCEPTING THE THINGS I CANNOT CHANGE; I'M CHANGING THE THINGS I CANNOT ACCEPT

1. What did I study in college?
   A. Medicine
   B. Business
   C. Pre-Law
2. What association was I the chairman of?
   A. NAACP
   B. BPP
   C. SNCC
3. What is the name of the alliance I created?
   A. Rainbow Coalition
   B. Treaty of Alliance
   C. Alliance for Progress

Fredrick Hampton
Answers

14th amendment answers
1) State governments
2) People that participated in a rebellion
3) Freed slaves
4) You were born in the U.S.
5) Signed into law
6) three fifths

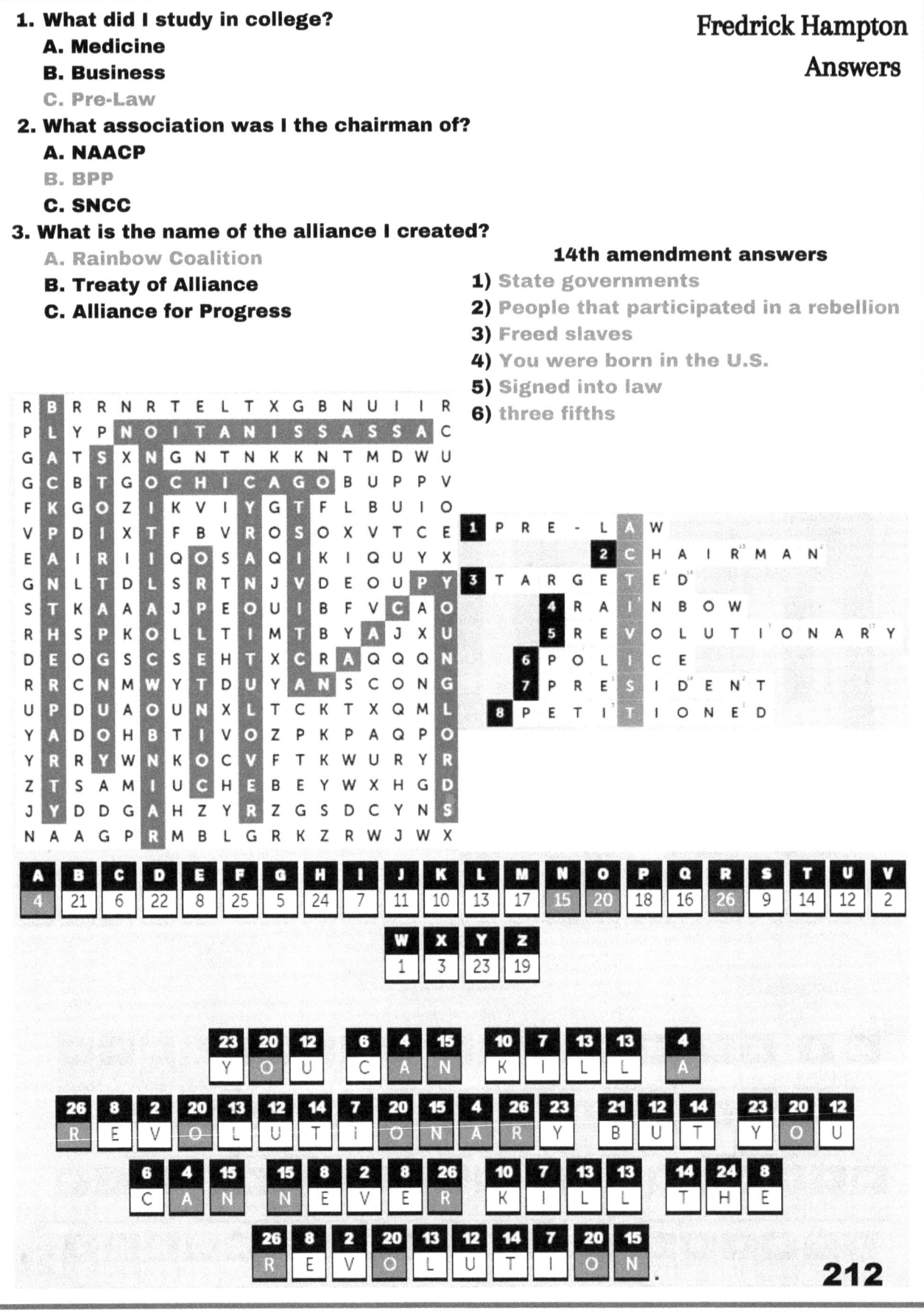

YOU CAN KILL A REVOLUTIONARY BUT YOU CAN NEVER KILL THE REVOLUTION.

212

1. What college did I graduate from?
   A. University of Illinois
   B. Fisk University
   C. NC A&T University
2. What sport did I get a scholarship for?
   A. Baseball
   B. Basketball
   C. Football
3. What organization didn't I create?
   A. Rainbow Coalition
   B. SCLC
   C. PUSH

Jesse Jackson
Answers

213

Dorothy Height Answers

1. What is my Master's Degree in?
   A. Politics
   B. Criminal Justice
   C. Educational Psychology
2. What year did I become the president of NCNW?
   A. 1990
   B. 1958
   C. 1947
3. What sorority am I apart of?
   A. Alpha Kapa Alpha
   B. Sigma Gamma Rho
   C. Delta Sigma Theta

Dorothy adjectives answers will vary.

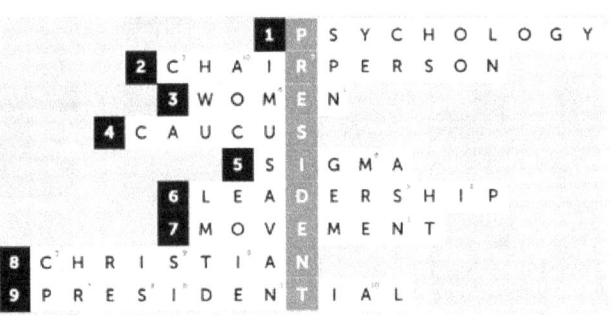

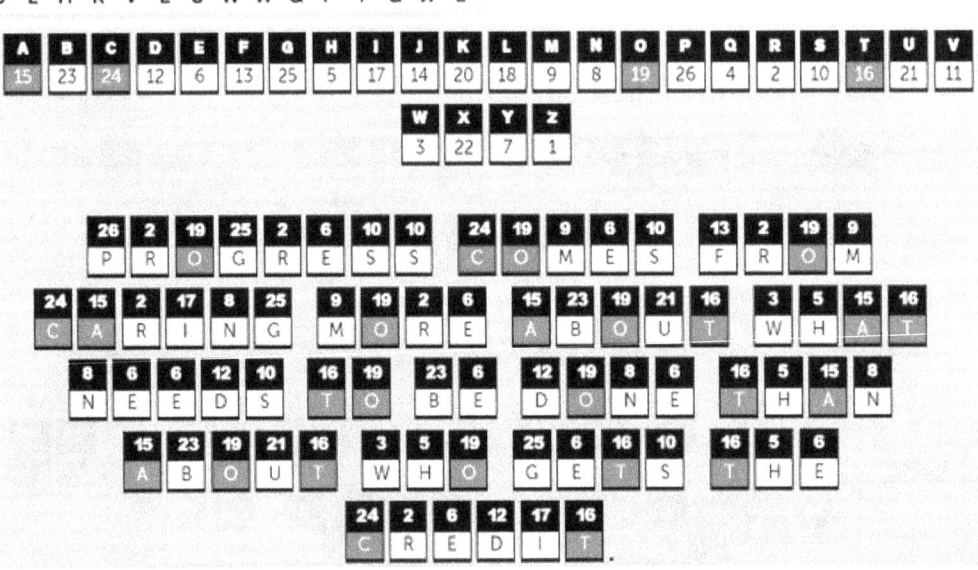

"PROGRESS COMES FROM CARING MORE ABOUT WHAT NEEDS TO BE DONE THAN ABOUT WHO GETS THE CREDIT."

214

Malcolm Little Answers

1. **What did I go to prison for?**
   A. Larceny
   B. Murder
   C. Kidnapping
2. **What year did I become a member of Nation of Islam?**
   A. 1946
   B. 1948
   C. 1950
3. **What Temple was I selected to lead?**
   A. Temple Number 1
   B. Temple Number 11
   C. Temple Number 7

Nation of Islam answers

1) Fasting
2) Five Pillars of Islam
3) A text describing the actions and sayings of Muhammad
4) Muslims
5) Submission
6) Towards the city of Mecca
7) The holy book of Islam

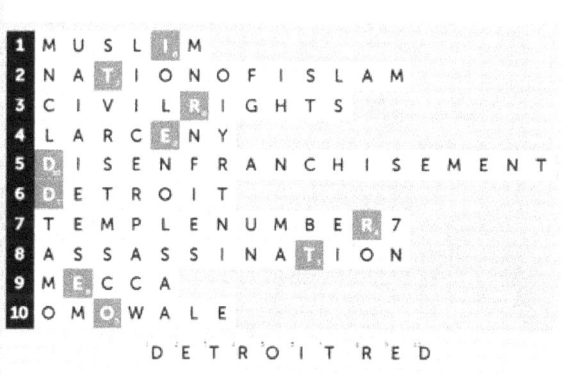

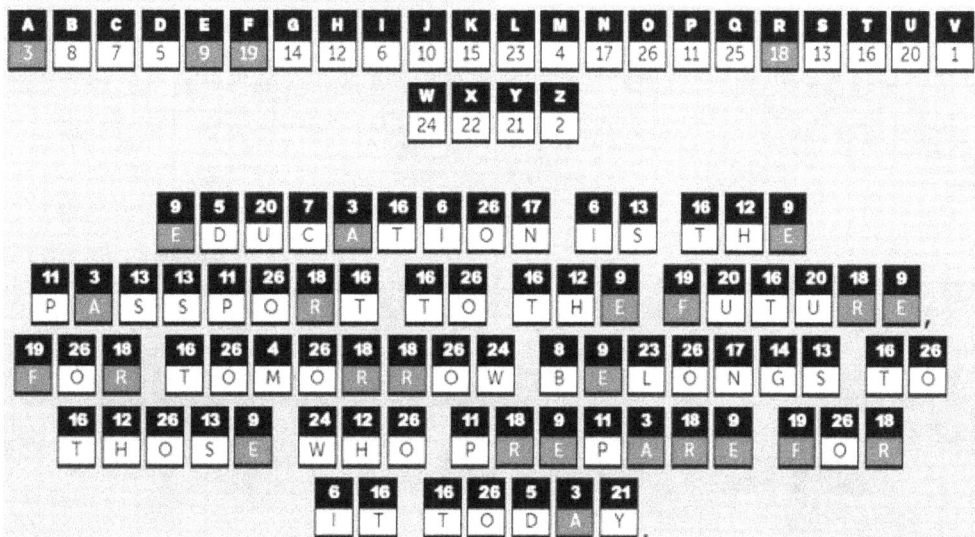

"EDUCATION IS THE PASSPORT TO THE FUTURE, FOR TOMORROW BELONGS TO THOSE WHO PREPARE FOR IT TODAY."

Kamala D. Harris
Answers

1. What Sorority am I a member of?
   A. Zeta Phi Beta
   B. Alpha Kappa Alpha
   C. Delta Sigma Theta
2. What college did I get my Juris Doctor from?
   A. Howard University
   B. Berkley University
   C. University of California
3. I was the first women in U.S. history receive this title?
   A. President
   B. Vice President
   C. Sectary of Defense

Presidential and Vice President responsibilities answers
1) True
2) Vice President
3) 15
4) To take over as president if the president dies or can no longer do the job of president
5) The power to break a tie vote in the Senate
6) The Supreme Court
7) All of the above

YOU NEVER HAVE TO ASK ANYONE'S PERMISSION TO LEAD. JUST LEAD.

216

Medgar Evers Answers

1. What Branch of Service did I serve in?
   A. U.S. Marine Corps
   B. U.S. Army
   C. U.S. Navy
2. What HBCU did I go to?
   A. Alcorn State University
   B. Alabama State University
   C. Southern University
3. What college did I help integrate?
   A. Ole Miss
   B. Mississippi State University
   C. Alcorn State University

Government for the State answers
1) Taxes
2) The Judicial
3) Chief Justice
4) Sales tax
5) Property tax
6) The governor

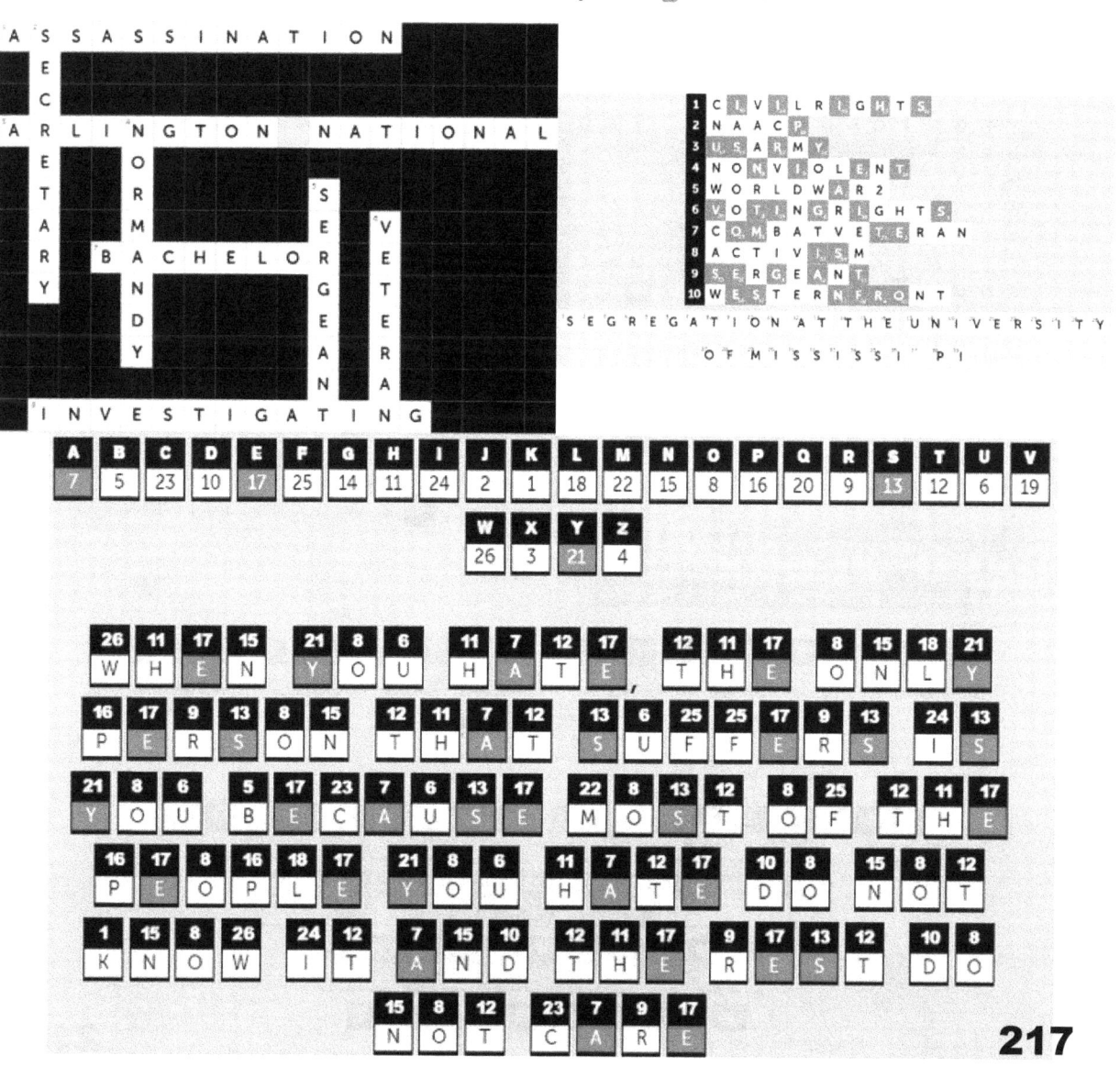

"WHEN YOU HATE, THE ONLY PERSON THAT SUFFERS IS YOU BECAUSE MOST OF THE PEOPLE YOU HATE DO NOT KNOW IT AND THE REST DO NOT CARE"

Colin Kaepernick Answers

1. What college did I get my degree from?
   A. UCLA
   B. University of Wisconsin
   C. University of Nevada
2. What year did I get drafted to the 49ers?
   A. 2011
   B. 2009
   C. 2012
3. What organization did I help found?
   A. NAACP
   B. Know Your Rights Camp
   C. National Urban League

Bill of rights answers
1) Fals
2) All of the above.
3) John Adams
4) The first
5) The Constitution
6) The right to choose not to testify against oneself
7) The first 10

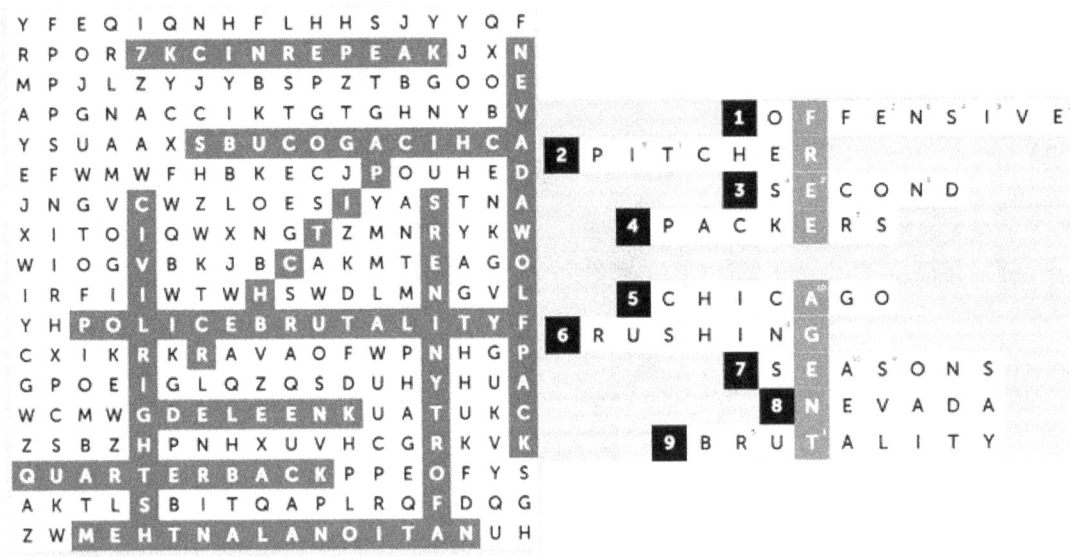

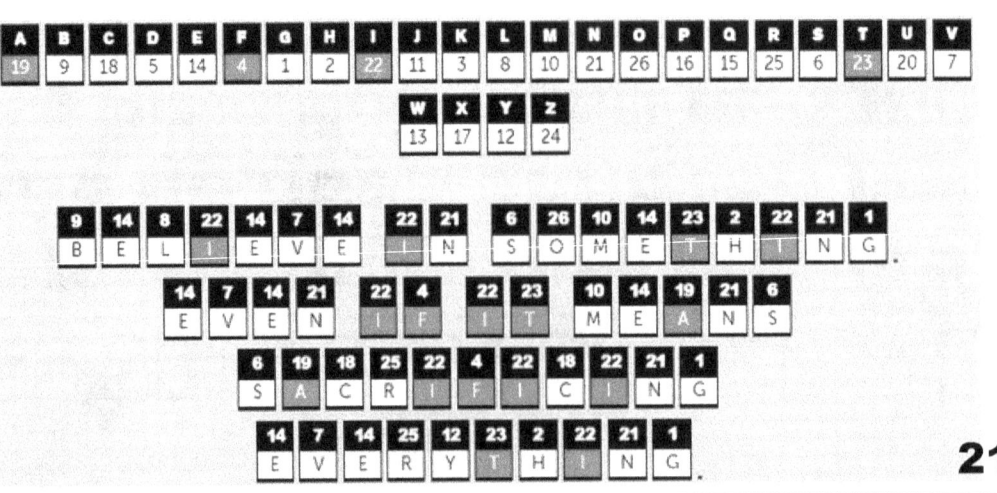

218

Rolihlahla Mandela
Answers

1. What was my Bachelor's degree in?
   A. Politics
   B. Medical
   C. Law
2. What year did I become president of South Africa?
   A. 1967
   B. 1990
   C. 1994
3. What did I negotiate to end?
   A. Apartheid
   B. Sex Trafficking
   C. Smuggling

Nelson facts answers

1) 1993
2) July 18th
3) African National Congress
4) A government system where people were separated by the color of their skin
5) 27 years
6) Law
7) False

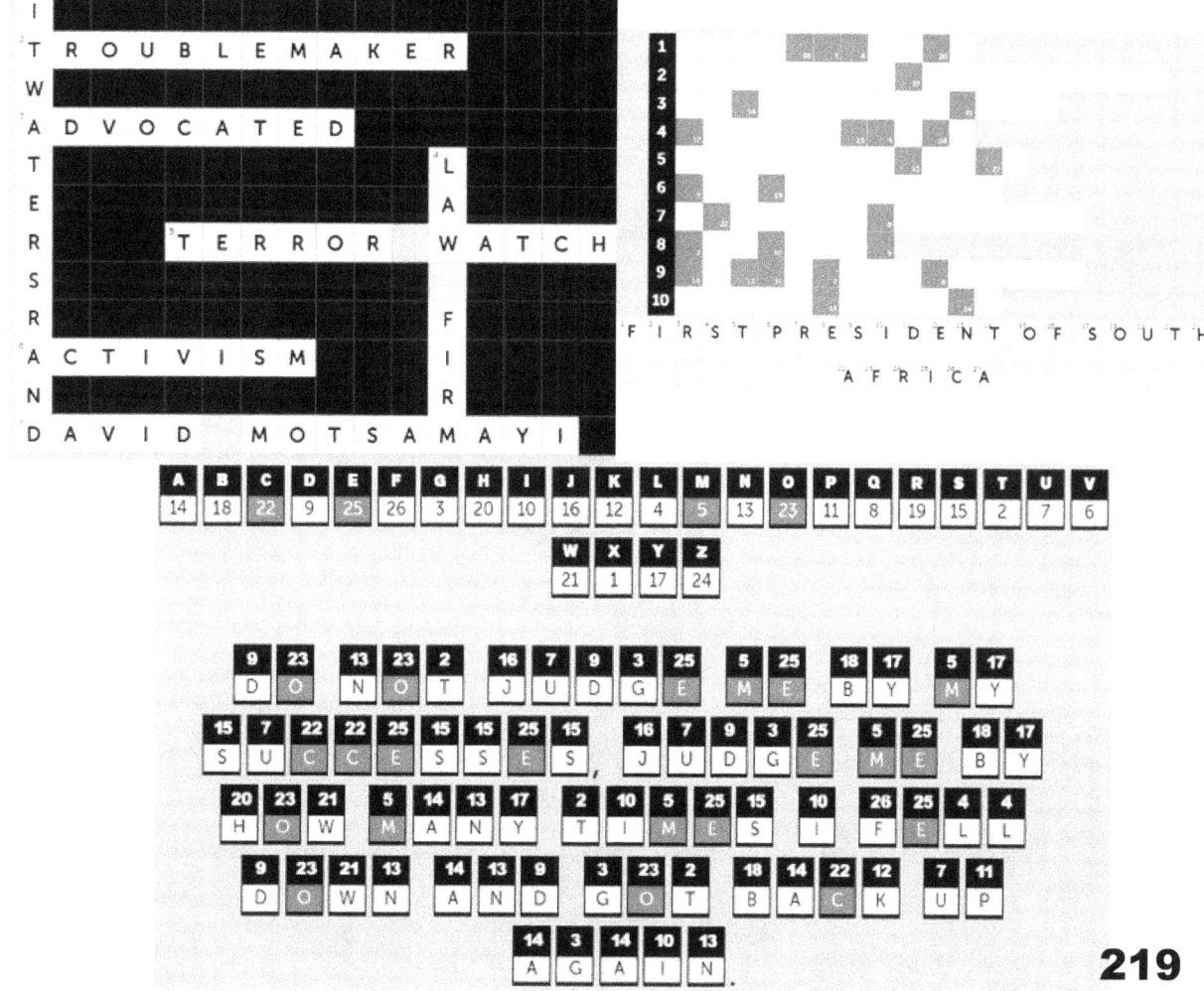

"DO NOT JUDGE ME BY MY SUCCESSES, JUDGE ME BY HOW MANY TIMES I FELL DOWN AND GOT BACK UP AGAIN."

219

Rosa Parks Answers

1. What was I able to do in 1945?
   A. Ride the bus in any seat
   B. Vote
   C. Join the Military
2. What year did I join the civil rights movement?
   A. 1943
   B. 1950
   C. 1944
3. When was the law passed to segregate the buses?
   A. 1943
   B. 1920
   C. 1900

Bus Boycott answers
1) $10
2) Alabama
3) NAACP
4) Shoes
5) They boycotted by refusing to ride the city buses
6) Over a year

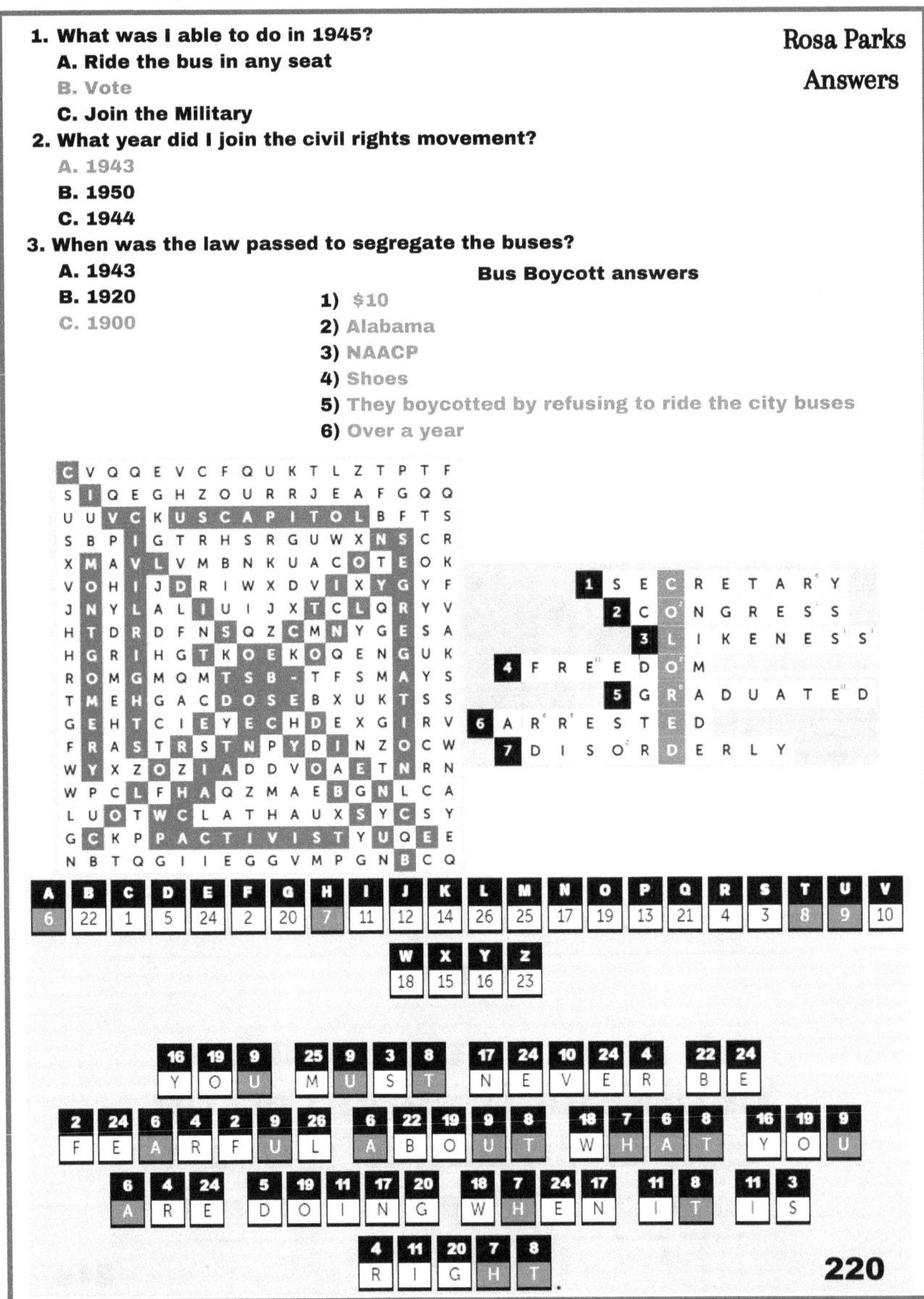

YOU MUST NEVER BE
FEARFUL ABOUT WHAT YOU
ARE DOING WHEN IT IS
RIGHT.

220

Thurgood Marshall Answers

1. What fraternity am I a member of?
   A. Omega Psi Phi
   B. Kappa Alpha Psi
   C. Alpha Phi Alpha
2. What year did I get confirmed to the Supreme Court?
   A. 1967
   B. 1961
   C. 1965
3. What college is my BA in literature and philosophy?
   A. Howard University
   B. Lincoln University
   C. Fisk University

Thurgood answers
1) Laurence Fishburne
2) NAACP
3) Lyndon Johnson
4) Brown v. Board of Education
5) John F. Kennedy
6) Tom C. Clark

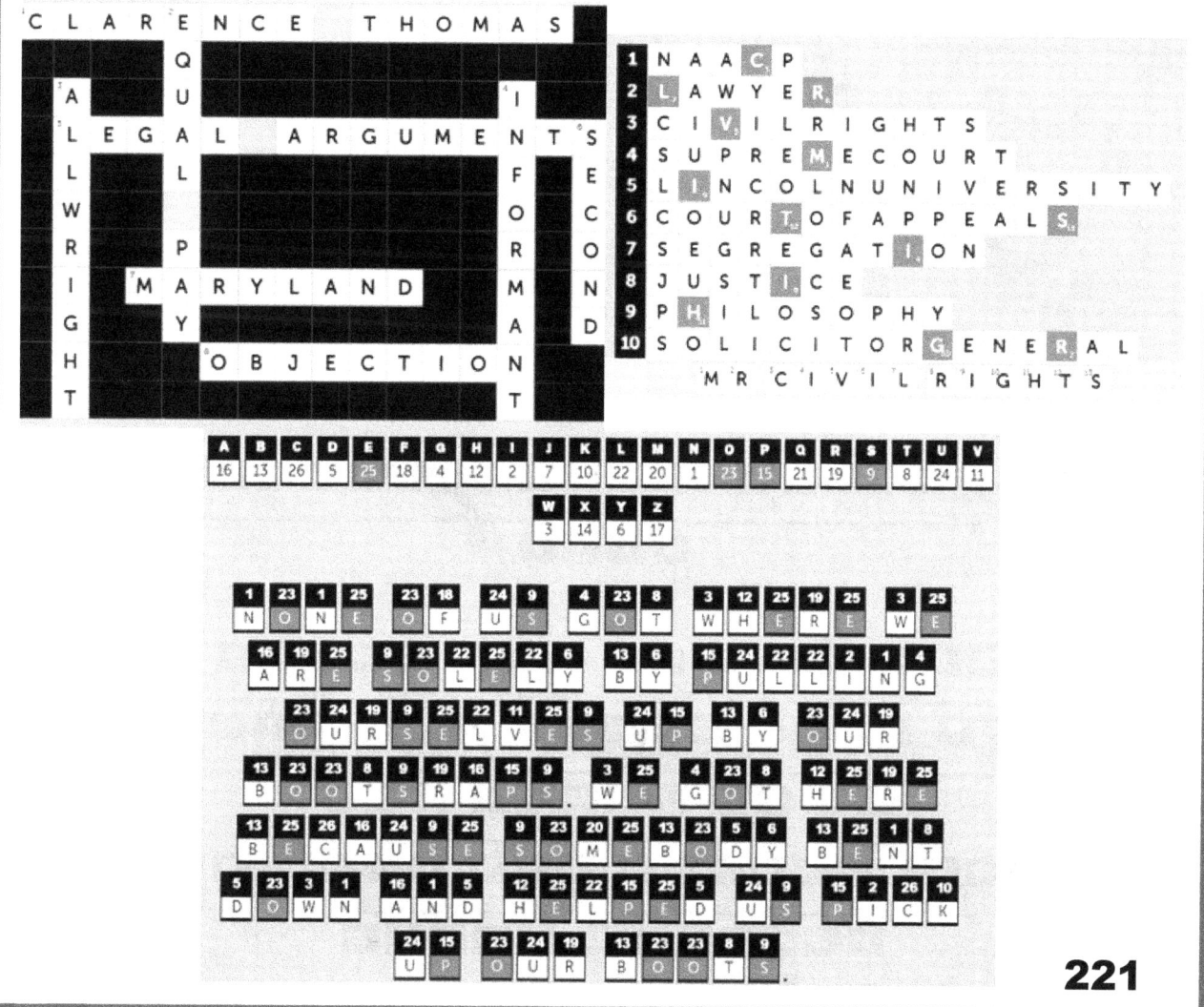

Crossword answers:
- CLARENCE THOMAS
- A QUILL
- LEGAL ARGUMENTS
- ALL WRIGHT
- PLAYBOY
- MARYLAND
- IFORMAT / ECONDFORMAT
- OBJECTION

1. NAACP
2. LAWYER
3. CIVIL RIGHTS
4. SUPREME COURT
5. LINCOLN UNIVERSITY
6. COURT OF APPEALS
7. SEGREGATION
8. JUSTICE
9. PHILOSOPHY
10. SOLICITOR GENERAL

MR CIVIL RIGHTS

Cryptogram: "None of us got where we are solely by pulling ourselves up by our bootstraps. We got here because somebody bent down and helped us pick up our boots."

Michelle Obama
Answers

1. What college did I get my Juris Doctor from?
   A. Princeton University
   B. Harvard University
   C. Colombia University
2. What University did I work for?
   A. Illinois
   B. New York
   C. Chicago
3. I was the first African-American female to what?
   A. Become President of the United States
   B. Become Vice President of the United States
   C. Become First Lady of the United States

Let's move answers
1) National School Lunch Program
2) cookies
3) True
4) Eleanor Roosevelt
5) Sixty minutes of physical activity a day
6) True

Crossword:
1. FRENCH-FRIES
2. COMMUNITY
3. CORPORATE
4. SECOND
5. DEVELOPMENT
6. SOCIOLOGY
7. INITIATIVE
8. ADVOCATE
9. OBESITY

(Down: FIRST LADY)

SUCCESS IS NOT ABOUT HOW MUCH MONEY YOU MAKE. IT IS ABOUT THE DIFFERENCE YOU MAKE IN PEOPLE'S LIVES.

222

1. What college didn't I go to?
   A. Boston University
   B. Morehouse College
   C. Clark University
2. What age did I get my Ph.D in systematic theology?
   A. 35
   B. 40
   C. 25
3. What organization did I help found?
   A. SCLC
   B. NAACP
   C. SNCC

Michael King
Answers

Civil Rights answers
1) Jim Crow
2) Civil Rights Act
3) Voter's Rights Act
4) True
5) Thirteenth Amendment

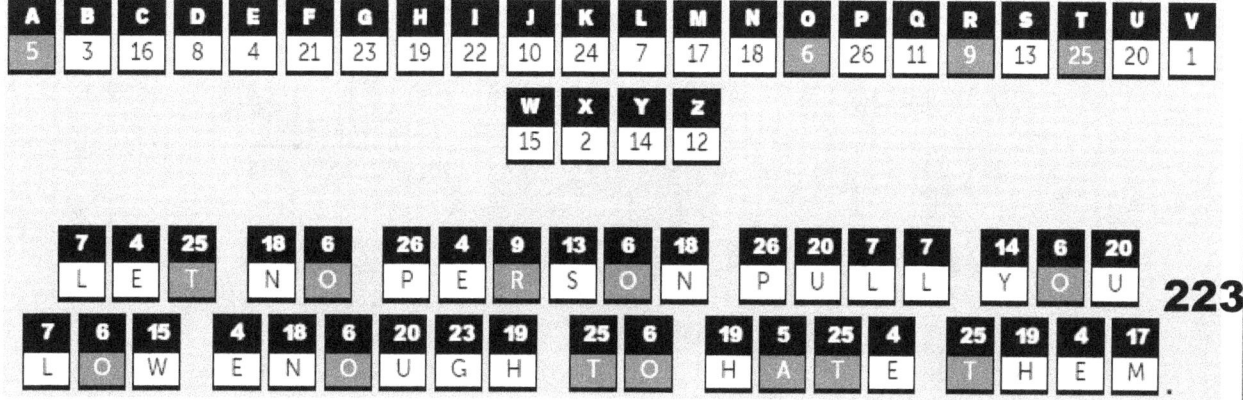

"LET NO PERSON PULL YOU LOW ENOUGH TO HATE THEM."

Isabella Baumfree
Answers

1. My name before I changed it to Sojourner Truth was?
   A. Sophia Baumfree
   B. Elizabeth Baumfree
   C. Isabella Baumfree
2. What year did I escape being a slave?
   A. 1826
   B. 1821
   C. 1825
3. I was one of the first black women to do what?
   A. Become a free person
   B. Own a house
   C. Win a court case against a white man

Sojourner speeches answers
1) Sang a song
2) Boston
3) Three
4) Hissing and Groaning
5) Abolitionist

Crossword Answers:
1. DUTCH
2. PATHFINDER
3. CIVIL
4. WOMAN
5. LINCOLN
6. SIGNIFICANT
7. RELIEF
8. ALABAMA
9. SLAVERY

Cipher Key:
A	B	C	D	E	F	G	H	I	J	K	L	M	N	O	P	Q	R	S	T	U	V	W	X	Y	Z
2	23	13	26	10	25	18	9	20	16	22	4	11	7	5	6	1	8	12	19	21	14	3	17	24	15

Decoded message:
"I WILL NOT ALLOW MY LIFE'S LIGHT TO BE DETERMINED BY THE DARKNESS AROUND ME."

224

Huey Newton
Answers

1. What is the highest education I achieved?
   A. Masters Degree
   B. Ph.D
   C. Bachelors Degree
2. What is the name of my fraternity?
   A. Phi Beta Sigma
   B. Omega Psi Phi
   C. Kappa Alpha Psi
3. What city was the Free Breakfast for Children Program?
   A. Oakland
   B. San Francisco
   C. Fresno

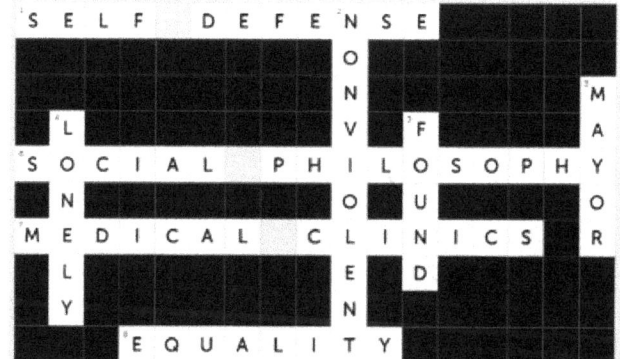

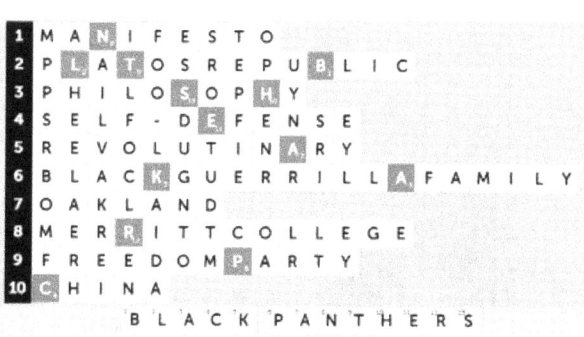

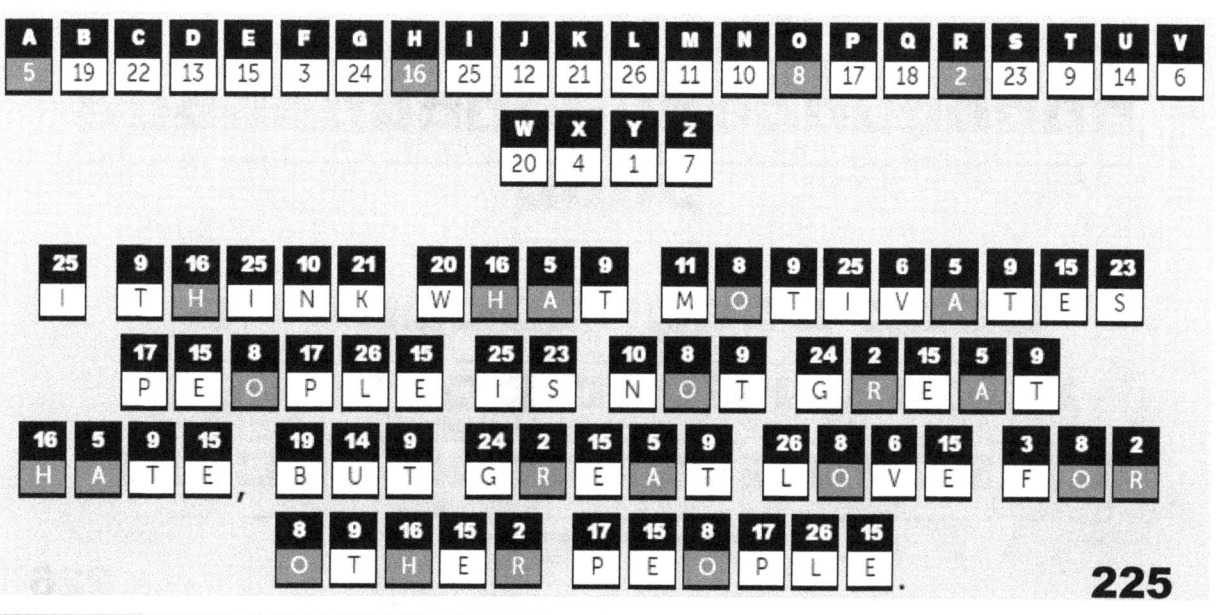

"I THINK WHAT MOTIVATES PEOPLE IS NOT GREAT HATE, BUT GREAT LOVE FOR OTHER PEOPLE."

225

1. What University did I get my Juris Doctorate from?
   A. State University of New York
   B. New York University
   C. City University of New York
2. What did I do before I appeared on Oprah's Show?
   A. Day time TV
   B. Radio
   C. Movies
3. What city was I a Public Defender in?
   A. Philadelphia
   B. Brooklyn
   C. Manhattan

Rhonda Harris
Answers

Public speaking answers
1) Answers will vary
2) Answers will vary
3) Answers will vary
4) True
6) Conclusion

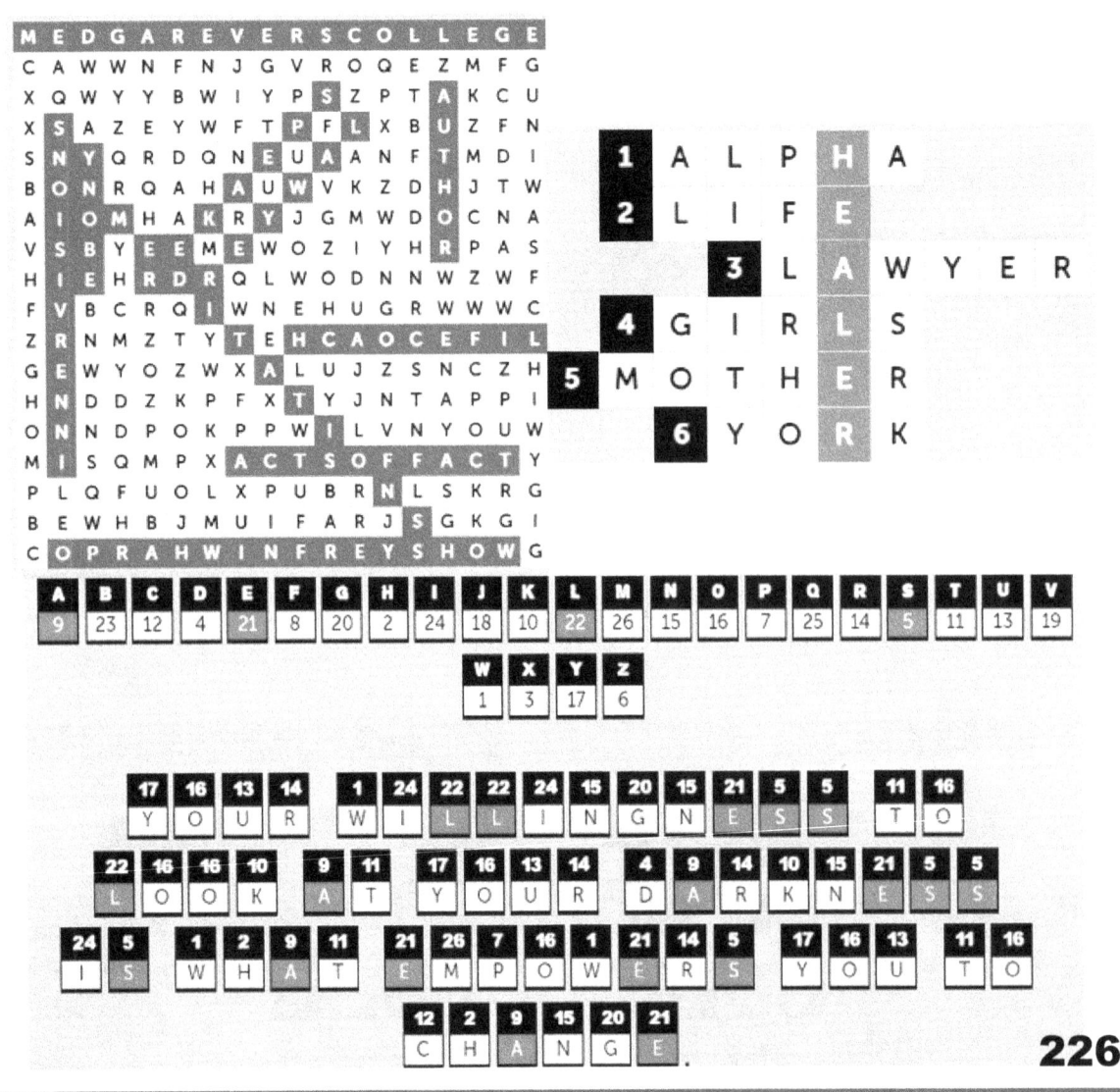

226

1. What was the name of my court case?
   A. Colvin v. Montgomery
   B. Austin v. Colvin
   C. Browder v Gayle
2. What did the local's do when I got convicted?
   A. Protest at the Police Station
   B. Boycott the Police Station
   C. Boycott the Bus System
3. What did the bus boycott become known as?
   A. Rosa Parks Movement
   B. Montgomery Bus Boycott
   C. Browder v. Gayle

Claudette Austin

Answers

Browder v. Gayle facts
1) Judge Kristi DuBose
2) Five
3) 381 days
4) December 17, 1956
5) W. A. Gayle

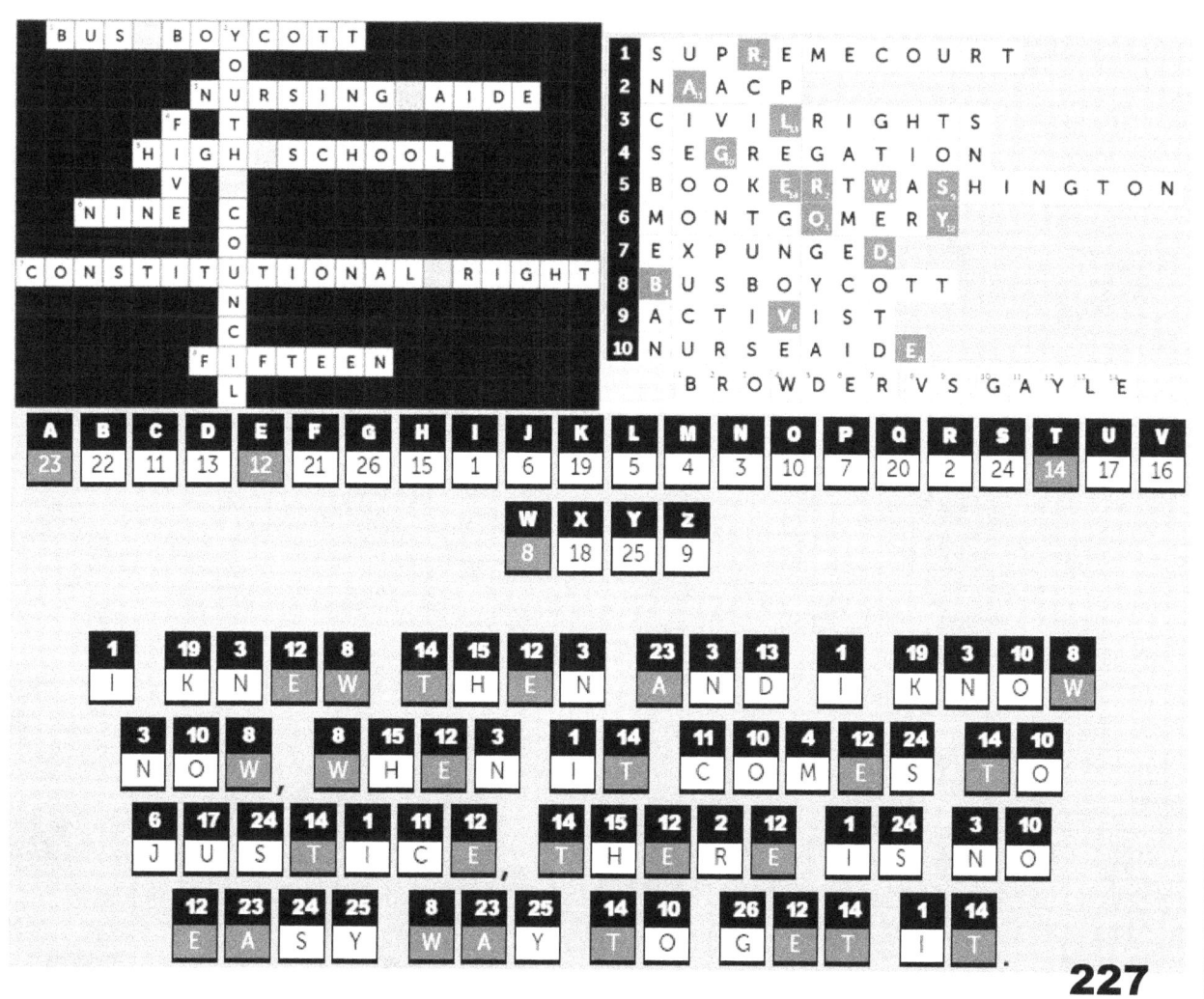

I KNEW THEN AND I KNOW NOW, WHEN IT COMES TO JUSTICE, THERE IS NO EASY WAY TO GET IT.

This book is dedicated to my grandkids
Anais Isabella Pablo-Antonio
Deyshawn Frank Chambers
Alicia Marie Jackson
Ayianna Marie Chambers
Zion Jamaris Jackson
Jayvon Jerome Jackson

ABOUT THE AUTHOR

Matthew D. Hale, the author of Black Historical Figures is a retired Marine and disabled veteran. He received his Bachelor of Arts in Computer Science from Campbell University and his Master of Science in Computer Engineering from Boston University. Matthew spends his down time making music, traveling, playing, and developing his own video games. Follow Matthew on Facebook/Meta at wegonnalearntoday, Instagram @ w_g_l_t and Tic Tok at wegonnalearntoday. Go to wegonnalearntoday.com or everydollarcountz.com for additional information.

In 2020 Matthew developed an interactive website, www.wegonnalearntoday, to provide access to Black History through games, music and videos. The website grew into the Black Historical Figures workbook series as a way to supplement the black history curricula taught in the school systems.

'In order to grow you must visit uncomfortable places'

10 BOOK SERIES
RELEASE DATES

NOVEMBER 2022

FEBRUARY 2023

MAY 2023

AUGUST 2023

NOVEMBER 2023

GET YOUR COPY TODAY
DON'T FORGET TO TELL A FRIEND

www.ingramcontent.com/pod-product-compliance
Lightning Source LLC
Chambersburg PA
CBHW080335170426
43194CB00014B/2573